MW01096482

Just Breathe
(and Take a Sip of Coffee)

HOMESCHOOL IN STEP *with* GOD

Carrie DeFrancisco

@coffeewithcarrie.org

Isaiah 54:13

Just Breathe (and Take a Sip of Coffee): Homeschool in Step with God
Copyright © 2020 by Carrie De Francisco. All rights reserved. This publication may not be reproduced, copied, or recorded by any means in part or whole without the prior permission of the author and publisher, except for the brief quotations in side boxes. When quotes are used, author's name or coffeewithcarrie must be cited.

For more information, visit Coffee With Carrie online at coffeewithcarrie.org

Cover photograph of coffee cup by Canva ©. All rights reserved.
Cover design by Coffeewithcarrie ©. All rights reserved.

Unless otherwise indicated, all Scripture quotations are taken from the New International Version (NIV),® copyright © 1973, 1978, 1984, 2011 by Biblica, Inc.®. All rights reserved worldwide.

Scripture quotations marked NLT are taken from the Holy Bible, New Living Translation, copyright © 1996, 2004, 2015 by Tyndale House Foundation. Carol Stream, Illinois, 60188. All rights reserved.

Copyright © 2020 Carrie De Francisco
All rights reserved.
ISBN: 9798652002282

Dedication

To my best friend and husband,

Thank you for living, loving, and learning alongside me.

And to my precious gifts, Francesca and Joseph,

Your unconditional love, never-ending patience,

and constant encouragement have made being

your mom and your teacher the best adventures of my life.

May you continue to follow your heart and to follow Jesus.

4

Table of Contents

INTRODUCTION

In my heart I feel you say,
Just breathe, just breathe.
Come and rest at my feet,
And be, just be.
Chaos calls but all you really need is to just
breathe.

~Johnny Diaz, "Breathe"

7

Just breathe… Take a deep breath. Exhale. Sip a cup of coffee. It is going to be alright. Trust me, friend. We have all been where you are right now. As a matter of fact, some of us have been there on multiple occasions and in multiple seasons. I have been there so many times, I stopped counting. It is the nature of the beast. The gift of motherhood is a blessing, but those little miniature versions of you can also be a challenge. If you have also been called to homeschool, then your blessings and challenges have just been kicked up a notch!

Sometimes, we need someone to come alongside us and remind us to *just breathe*. We need someone to reassure us it is going to be ok. Sometimes, we just need someone who understands the rolling around on the floor when the word math is mentioned, or someone who can relate to leaving the house while wearing your shirt inside out (True story… on multiple occasions!) It's a gift when you find someone who understands your coffee mug has been in the microwave for five hours, or someone who understands why your coffee mug is in the freezer and frozen bananas are in the kitchen drawer (True story… again). Sometimes we just need someone who has "been there, done that" to come alongside us and give us permission to stop. No, you can't stop being a mom (for better or worse those little eating machines are yours forever and there is no such thing as early retirement). However, I do mean you have permission to stop the crazy train you call your week to rest, refresh, and refocus. Actually, we not only have permission, we have a mandate to do just that.

God commanded us (not suggested or recommended) but commanded us to take a sabbath day, a day to rest. *"Remember the Sabbath day by keeping it holy. Six days you shall labor and do all your work, but the seventh day is a sabbath to the Lord your God. On it you shall not do any work. For in six days the Lord made the heavens and the earth, the sea, and all that is in them, but he rested on the seventh day. Therefore the Lord blessed the Sabbath day and made it holy"* (Exodus 20:8-11 NIV). Taking a day to rest the mind, body, and heart is important to our Heavenly Father. God knows what is best for us. He knows without rest we will eventually run out of steam, which will ultimately harm ourselves and quite possibly harm those around us. Am I also giving you permission to stop homeschooling? Well, no. If God has called you to homeschool, then you should continue the adventure. However,

"Remember the Sabbath day by keeping it holy. Six days you shall labor and do all your work, but the seventh day is a sabbath to the Lord your God."

Exodus 20:8:11

it is extremely important to also follow the principles of the Sabbath while homeschooling. Happy Mama, happy family!

Just breathe…. Take another deep breath. Exhale slowly. Sip a little more coffee. Put your feet up and let's take a little break to talk about slowing down, stopping, and simplifying. As Solomon exhorted in the Book of Ecclesiastes, there is nothing new under the sun (1:9). While reading this book, you may find a few "ah ha" moments about being a mother and about being a homeschooling mom, but what I hope you will mostly discover are important reminders about motherhood and much needed encouragement about homeschooling. While there is nothing new under the sun and no huge revelation I can give you about this 24/7 job we call homeschooling, we all do experience different seasons in life, in marriage, in motherhood, and in home education. In the pages of this book, you will find many tried and true reminders and tips I have either learned from homeschooling masters such as Sally Clarkson and Carol Joy Seid, or ideas I have implemented in my own homeschooling through experimentation and experience. Ecclesiastes also reminds us, *"To every thing there is a season, and a time to every purpose under the heaven"* (3:1). There is a season to plant and a season to sow, a season to break down and a season to build up, a time to weep and a time to laugh, a time to keep and time to cast out, and a time to keep silent and a time to speak up.

Depending on the season you find yourself, the message in this book may be brand new. Perhaps you are new to homeschooling and no one has ever told you it's ok to skip the big homeschool convention, the overwhelming exhibit hall, and all the fancy boxed curriculums. Perhaps you have never been told that you can simply learn together at home without all the extra bells and whistles. If you are new to homeschooling, you will be relieved to read in these pages permission to slow down, to stop on occasion, and to simplify your days. As you read, you might find yourself breathing a huge sigh of relief.

To those sojourners who have been on this homeschooling journey for a while, you are probably in a different season of motherhood and a different season of homeschooling than you were just a few years ago. The words on these pages may not be new to you, but they might just be the reminders you need to hear right now. You may find words of encouragement you are desperately seeking and needing to hear.

My Bible is full of highlighted passages, notes in the margins, and prayers squeezed in between the texts, but it never fails. As my 52 year old eyes read my old tattered Bible, I usually come across a verse that isn't highlighted and I think to myself, "Girl, why didn't you commit that verse to memory?! Why didn't you highlight this one years ago?" Simply put, back then I wasn't in the season I'm in right now. As I read God's Word now, it speaks to my more mature version of myself in a different way. As I read particular verses now, they didn't speak to me ten years ago like they do today. I couldn't relate to a particular passage twenty years ago. But now? Oh yes! I get it now as I read these same overlooked and neglected verses. Now, the words are like daggers to my heart, or they are words that soothe my broken heart. God knows what we need when we need it. Today as I read parts of the Old Testament or some of the new Testament, God allows the scales to fall from my eyes so I can see, I mean really see, the promises He has for me now, this year, and in this season. I pray you will have the same experience as you read this book. I hope the encouragement on these pages are what you need to hear right now in this season of your life and in this part of your homeschooling journey.

Not only do I have those "ah ha" moments while reading my Bible, but I find I do the same thing with some of my favorite homeschool "go to" books. While I have never met some of my homeschooling mentors in person, I have looked to them for wisdom, reassurance, and encouragement the past twenty years of homeschooling. I have met them in the pages of their books or while listening to their podcasts. I can read and reread books written by homeschool giants like Dr. Raymond Moore and Sally Clarkson over and over again, and each time, I find some new nugget of truth every time I peruse the pages of their books. Simply put, I am in a different season of life and homeschooling when I read God's Word or a classic homeschool "how to" book. I have a different set of challenges. My family might be larger (or smaller). My circumstances might be different. My location might be new.

There truly is nothing new under the sun. Some of the sage advice in this book are tried and true things I have implemented over the years because they were suggested by a pillar in the homeschool community. Some have been suggested to me by veteran homeschool moms who are now reaping the rewards of being a grandmother while helping to raise a second generation of homeschoolers. Some have been revealed to me through experience, through Holy Spirit nudges, and a few were even hair-brained ideas induced by a 1:00 PM coffee high. (The Lord does work in mysterious ways!) I've tried to fill these pages with advice I have been given and with things I have done the past twenty years that I feel will bless you, encourage you, and help you to *just breathe*.

In *Just Breathe (and Take a Sip of Coffee)*, we will explore together how to homeschool in step with God. Together, we will explore how to rest in the Lord and simplify our homeschooling. We will explore how to regain our sanity, reclaim our schedules, and reignite our love for homeschooling through two straightforward and manageable principles: (1) The Sabbath Principle and (2) The Simplification Principle.

So grab your favorite cup of joe, get comfy, (sneak into the bathroom if needed to get a little peace and quiet), and *just breathe.*

PART ONE:
THE SABBATH PRINCIPLE

"By the seventh day, God had finished the work he had been doing so on the seventh day he rested from all his work.

Then God blessed the seventh day and made it holy, because on it he rested from all the work of creating that he had done."

Genesis 2:2-3 NIV

CHAPTER 1

Sabbath Day: A Day of Rest

Growing up, Sundays were "donut date day" with my dad. The two of us were the early risers in the family, so my dad would take me to Tastee Donuts (it's a southern thing) every Sunday morning. He would sip his chicory coffee, and I would eat my cream-filled chocolate-covered eclair. Some Sundays, he would read his paper while I read the comics. Some Sundays he read the comics to me. When I was older (and my dad's body was weaker), we would skip Tastee Donuts and stay home for coffee and conversation. We often talked about politics, the headlines in the newspaper, or how things were going in my life. I think part of my obsession with coffee is because of the fond memories I have sharing coffee with my Dad every Sunday morning. There is nothing like the smell of chicory coffee to put me in my happy (and safe) place.

We never missed church on Sunday either. After my dad and I had our coffee and donuts, we would watch my mom and brother slowly grumble their way around the house to get ready for church. Both my brother and mom were not morning people. It was an unspoken rule: Do not speak to them until spoken to. Somehow our Sunday morning ritual always ended up with my dad aggravated and blowing the car horn because we were taking too long. My mom hated to be late for church but getting up and out of the house on Sunday mornings were a killer for her. But church was a priority for her. Sundays just weren't Sundays without donuts, coffee, and church.

Coming from an Italian southern family, Sundays also meant family supper at our house, which was usually homemade red gravy (that's tomato sauce for you non-southerners), meatballs and spaghetti. If I was lucky, eggplant or veal parmesan was also on the

We need time to be with family, to be with friends, to be with God in Worship, to rest, and to just be.

Sunday menu! My mama's red gravy was to die for. She would start cooking it before we left for church and this Italian magic would grace our plates (and enter our tummies) by 3:00. It was important to my mom that we honored the Sabbath on Sundays. My dad didn't work on Sundays (or at least he tried to avoid the phone messages calling him in to fix some problem). My mom didn't do laundry or shop. (Back then in the South, none of the stores were open on Sundays anyway.) My brother and I humbly obliged by not catching up on any homework we may have purposely or inadvertently forgotten to do on Friday.

Anything for mom, right?! We had to be home too. We had to eat together as a family. We could invite as many friends over as we wanted (and of course all were welcome at the table), but we were to be home as a family on Sundays. Our Sunday afternoons were usually full of Saints football, card games, more newspaper reading, and a few naps in-between games and meal time. Back then, I didn't appreciate what my mom and dad were doing. They were instilling in my brother and me the importance of taking time each week to rest and to just be. To be with family, to be with friends, and to be with God in worship. Even as we got older, our Sabbath may have looked different, but the pattern was still there: God, family, and rest.

God commanded Adam and Eve to rest. They were to take a day to *just be*. They were to take a day to ponder and appreciate the wonders that God created. They were to take a day to worship and thank God for the wonderful things He had given them. God later commanded the Israelites to do the same thing. In Deuteronomy 5:12-16, God reminded them, *"Observe the Sabbath day by keeping it holy, as the Lord your God has commanded you. Six days you shall labor and do all your work, but the seventh day is a sabbath to the Lord your God. On it you shall not do any work, neither you, nor your son or daughter, nor your male or female servant, nor your ox, your donkey or any of your animals, nor any foreigner residing in your towns, so that your male and female servants may rest, as you do."* It was important to God they not only take a day to rest and worship but to pass this commandment on to future generations. *"These commandments that I give you today are to be on your hearts. Impress them on your children. Talk about them when you sit at home and when you walk along the road, when you lie down and when you get up. Tie them as symbols on your hands and bind them on your foreheads. Write them on the door frames of your houses and on your gates"* (Deuteronomy 6: 6- 9 NIV). Little did I know but now as a mom I realize, my mom and dad were not only obeying the Sabbath ,but they were also passing on its importance to my brother and me.

By calling His people to observe the Sabbath and to observe holy days, God was making sure His people took time out of their busy schedules to remember who God was and what HE has done.

Later God instituted days of remembrance. God knows our sinful human nature. He knows that our hearts have a tendency to forget. By calling His people to observe the Sabbath and to observe holy days, God was making sure the people took time out of their busy schedules to remember who He was and what He does! Without taking a day to rest and worship, our hearts become ungrateful, our mouths begin to spew complaints, and our minds become overcrowded with pride. In our weariness, we blame God for our circumstances instead of praising Him for His many blessings. In our fifty plus hour weeks, we tend to believe it is our hard work that deserves praise not God's providential care. Because we are so tired and overworked, we fail to see God's fingerprints throughout our day and throughout our week. God knew if we did not set aside at least one day to reflect on His goodness and to meditate on His Word, we would lose our focus, our purpose, and our perspective.

God knew if we didn't set aside at least one day to reflect on His goodness and to meditate on His Word, we would lose our focus, our purpose, and our perspective.

I find the Mondays I despise the most come after a Sunday I didn't take a Sabbath! If my Monday begins with anger, grumbling, or feelings of disappointment, I can usually look back at the day before to understand why. Did I go to church? Did I do my grocery list and my week's "To Do List" while my pastor was preaching? Did I take time to really rest on Sunday? Did I spend time with family? Did I cease from the usual chores of the week? Did I take time to pray and thank God for the past week and to seek His guidance for the upcoming week? Did I serve my family, my church family, or my homeschool family? If I am lacking joy on Monday, it is usually because I answered "no" to one or some of these questions. The Lord promises you joy and to have joy in the Lord when you follow His Sabbath command. *"If you keep your feet from breaking the Sabbath and from doing as you please on my holy day, if you call the Sabbath a delight and the Lord's holy day honorable, and if you honor it by not going your own way and not doing as you please or speaking idle words, then you will find your joy in the Lord, and I will cause you to ride in triumph on the heights of the land and to feast on the inheritance of your father Jacob. For the mouth of the Lord has spoken"* (Isaiah 58: 13-14 NIV). I particularly enjoy *The Message* version of Isaiah 58:13-14. *"If you watch your step on the Sabbath and don't use my holy day for personal advantage, if you treat the Sabbath as a day of joy, God's holy day as a celebration, if you honor it by refusing business as usual making money, running here and there - Then you'll be free to enjoy God!* The NIV version reminds us our joy will be found in

"If you treat the Sabbath as a day of joy, God's holy day as a celebration...then you'll be free to enjoy God."

Isaiah 58: 13-14

the Lord. The Message version reminds us when we take a day of rest, we will have the time to enjoy the Lord!

If our desire is to homeschool in step with God and to enjoy this journey, our first lesson to learn is to truly honor the Sabbath and to take a day of rest. It is good for the heart, mind, body, and soul. It will help us fulfill our purpose for the rest of the week. It will help prepare our hearts and attitudes for the work God has set before us. It helps us seek God's will for the week. We need to truly set a day aside for rest and to worship and to follow the example set by the Israelites. In order to truly rest from work on the Sabbath, the Israelites prepared for it by getting things done the day before the Sabbath.

I know I feel behind and stressed when I wake up on Monday mornings with the realization I still have to plan for the day and the week. Because of this, I would spend every Sunday evening prepping lessons for our week. While it made my attitude on Monday mornings a bit more agreeable, it didn't give me a day to rest and to enjoy my family. Yes, we homeschool so we are spending time with our family and children seven days a week, but that doesn't mean the time we are spending with them is what I call "connecting" time. Can I connect with my child while doing Algebra lessons? Maybe, but not quite in a way my child needs to connect with me. Sure, we have had a few great mom/child moments over math lessons and Algebra instruction. I was a horrible math student and nearly failed math almost every year of my academic career, so I have been able to share some funny stories and some great life lessons learned during those math moments with my kids. But it isn't the "connecting time" I am longing to share with my children. Sometimes they just want and need time with me that isn't filled with worksheets or reading assignments. Our children just want us. They want our undivided attention. They want us fully present. The weekend, especially Sundays, are my favorite times to connect or reconnect with my kiddos. No lessons. No laundry. No catch up work. Just mom and family time. However, I was often so busy getting ready for the week's schoolwork that I neglected spending time with the family on the weekend. I can't tell you how many countless adventures I missed because I was home getting lessons ready while my husband and kids were driving to the snow or getting ice cream or visiting the Donut Man stand.

> *"On the sixth day, when they prepare what they bring in, it will be twice as much as they gather daily."*
>
> **Exodus 16:5**

In Exodus 16, God also instituted the concept of Double Portions. *"See, the Lord has given you the sabbath; therefore He gives you bread for two days on the sixth day"* (29). Since the Israelites were commanded to rest on the seventh day, God did not want them to do daily work on the Sabbath. When the Lord guides, He provides, so on the sixth day, God gave the Israelites double portions of manna. *"On the sixth day, when they prepare what they bring in, it will be twice as much as they gather daily"* (Exodus 16:5). They were to gather double portions on the sixth day so they would not have to gather on the Sabbath. Unlike other days, the manna did not spoil on the Sabbath Day. The Lord gave them exactly what they needed so they could truly rest on the Sabbath.

After studying the Book of Exodus, I was convicted to use this principle of double portions in our homeschooling. In an effort to truly enjoy the weekend and to honor the Sabbath, I began using Friday afternoons as my planning sessions. I took the lead of the Israelites. So now on Fridays after our lessons are complete, I sit down and plan our next week. One advantage to planning on Friday is the past week is fresh in my mind. I know what was accomplished, what is

Use the biblical principle of Double Portions in your homeschooling.

still in progress, and what needs to be tackled the next week. Another advantage is I have my list of things I have planned and supplies I don't have so if I am running errands or going to the grocery on Saturday, I can pick up what is needed. This approach has also made my Sunday evenings and Monday mornings less hectic. I'm not rushed to pick up a last minute item or to make copies of a worksheet late Sunday night. My favorite part of getting it all done Friday afternoon is I can jump into the weekend knowing I don't have a homeschool "to do list" hanging over my head. I can really enjoy the weekend and rest on the Sabbath.

Try to incorporate the Principle of Sabbath by taking a day to rest, to worship, and to have a "donut & coffee date" with your heavenly Father. Take the time and make the commitment to truly rest mentally, physically, and spiritually on the Sabbath. Incorporate the principle of Sabbath and Double Portions into your family time and homeschooling week by planning ahead on Fridays and spending time with your family on the weekends. For the rest of the week, you will *"find your joy in the Lord, and [He] will cause you to ride in triumph."*

CHAPTER 2
Sabbath Hour: An Hour of Rest

I have a confession to make. I am an extreme introvert. I didn't realize just how much I needed alone time to recharge until my first child was born. She is a talker, and I love that about her! She thinks out of the box, comes up with ideas to cheer up or help those around her, and consumes books like bears on honey. Because her mind is always in motion, her lips (at least when she was younger) were also in constant motion. It was at the 2:00 hour during her toddler and preschool years that I came to cherish nap time. I didn't realize how much I needed a little solitude, a little quiet, and a fresh cup of coffee until my daughter had snuggled up with her blanket for for a nap.

When she was a baby, I used her nap time as a time to catch up on things. Later, I realized I needed to use these moments to recharge instead. It wasn't much but an hour of Bible study, scrapbooking, or reading a good book was just what I needed to get through the rest of the afternoon and bedtime ritual later that evening. When my son was born, I really came to appreciate nap time because he didn't nap! You don't appreciate what you have until it's gone. While my daughter's mind was in constant motion, my son's body was in constant motion. My daughter mentally wore me out while my son physically wore me out. He would take a twenty minute cat nap here and there, but those naps were few and far between. He was my early riser too, so if I wanted some quiet time before the house was full of shuffling little feet and hungry little tummies, I had to get up before sunrise to beat my son. He did fall asleep relatively early in the evenings, but my daughter did not. She was and still is a night owl. I came to really appreciate the idea of quiet time or a sabbath hour.

When I first started homeschooling, a veteran mom insisted that the entire family have "quiet time" every afternoon after lunch. If the child was young enough for naps, he should sleep during quiet time. If the children were past the napping stage, they should stay in their rooms reading, resting, drawing, creating, or doing whatever they wanted to do as long as it didn't include talking or using an electronic device. I loved the idea! However, I tried for many seasons to implement this version of "quiet time," but it just didn't work quite the way it worked for my friend. While it fit her personality and her family's homeschool style, it just didn't fit ours.

We did, however, institute what I will now call our "Sabbath Hour," but it didn't necessarily happen right after lunch and we didn't all retreat to our rooms. My daughter would escape to her room to read one of her many novels or fantasy books while my son would build with Legos or play outside. I tried hard not to use my quiet time (or Sabbath Hour) to catch up on emails or make appointments. I made an effort to really rest. During these quiet moments, I would seek the Lord in prayer, read a book (usually on how to homeschool), or cook dinner. Let me explain. Cooking is a stress reliever for me. I am at my happiest when I am cooking or experimenting with a new recipe, so chopping onions or prepping a pot roast is actually quite relaxing for this introverted mama.

Without time each day to rest, relax, and create, we have a tendency to become grumpy little complainers.

I found over the years that if the kids and I didn't take some time each day to just rest, relax, or create, we were grumpy little complainers when my husband came home from work. I noticed the kids bickered with each other, or I had a very short temper. Whatever you want to call it- quiet time, nap time, alone time, or Sabbath time- it is a necessity in your homeschooling day. I know it is in mine. As an introvert, I need some alone time each day to regroup and recharge. I am better off and my family is better off for it. Even if you are an extrovert, make an effort to include a Sabbath Hour in your school day. It doesn't have to be long; an hour will do. At first, you may hear

"I'm bored" or "I don't know what to do," but those are my favorite things to hear as a homeschooling mom. Without electronics, sibling shenanigans, or organized play, your child is forced to find something to do. Some of my son's most creative drawings and my daughter's most creative ideas came after an hour of quiet time that started with "I'm bored."

You may be intrigued with the idea of inserting a Sabbath Hour into your school day, but you may not be sure how to start it, when to do it, or what to do during that time. It's never too late to start this practice, and there is no better time to start your Sabbath Hour than today. Prep your kiddos. Let them know what you will be doing and why. Give them ideas of what they can do during family quiet time and then just start. If your extreme extrovert can't stand being alone in his room, no problem. I have a child like that. I let my son hang out with me in the front room while I read or while I do my devotions. When he was younger, he would bring his drawing pad or Legos to wherever I was, and he would just chill with me. He would do his thing while I did mine.

It's never too late to start this practice, and there is no better time to start your Sabbath Hour than today.

The goal is to get them used to the idea that just for an hour each day, you want them to rest and relax. Over the years, I have found setting time aside mid-afternoon is the best time. If you have a large family or a family with older kids who have activities starting at 3:00 PM, then try taking some quiet time right after lunch. But it really doesn't matter what time you rest; the idea is to just make time to do it!

What to do during quiet time is strictly up to you and what works best for your family's personality. Some families love music so family members retreat to their rooms or different areas of the home with their headphones and listen to music. Some kids love to read or be read to so off they go to read a good book or listen to audible on their headsets. Antsy boys love to build so building blocks, Legos, and magnet-tiles are a great option. Creative kids love to draw, make things, sew, crochet, knit, and paint during Sabbath Hour. Older students sometimes take quiet time as their hour to do their own daily devotions or Bible study. Tired little ones can always go down for a nap. And there is nothing wrong with a teen taking a nap too. They are eating and growing machines. Sometimes a nap

Yet even Jesus, God the Son and Creator of the Universe, choose to take a break each day.

is just what a growing boy or hormonal girl needs to regroup and reassess their attitudes.

Jesus often took time to be alone. We see him praying, meditating, and even sleeping during these times. Jesus had many exhausting days. His days were filled with slow-learning disciples, hungry masses, sick and needy friends, and angry crowds. He was in constant demand all day long and sometimes for days on end. The people around him needed to be healed, to be fed, to be encouraged, and to be taught. Jesus was no stranger to dealing with friends and family like yours and like mine. If we think we are having a hard and hectic day, just imagine how exhausted and overwhelmed our Lord and Savior was. Yet even Jesus, God the Son and Creator of the Universe, chose to take a break each day. Jesus chose to rest when the disciples made their way across the Sea of Galilee. He stayed behind a few times to rest and pray while the disciples traveled to distant cities. Even in his most agonizing moments, we find Jesus alone in the garden praying and calling out to God in desperation. Even Jesus needed a little break each day. If you haven't already implemented some form of a Sabbath Hour into your homeschooling schedule, try incorporating it this school year.

CHAPTER 3

Sabbath Week: A Week of Rest

$\mathscr{I}$ love our Sabbath Weeks! I can't take credit for this life-changing idea. I was first introduced to taking a week off every six weeks of school time when our family participated in Classical Conservations (CC)®. Our community would meet and learn together for six weeks. Then in the seventh week, we took a break. At this time, I looked forward to our week off of classes so our family could spend time catching up on our other studies. In the beginning, we didn't really take a week to rest; we only took a week off from attending classes. It wasn't until I read *Teaching From Rest* by Sarah Mackenzie that I was reintroduced to this idea of a true Sabbath Week. I began to realize the true meaning of this much needed break. Sarah Mackenzie emphasizes the importance of truly taking a break from school work. It was such a radical idea for me. Take a whole week off to rest? Can we really afford to do that? Well, when our family began to really use our Sabbath Week to truly rest and regroup, our homeschooling radically changed for the better. I couldn't believe what a difference it made in my energy level, my children's work efforts, and our family's overall attitude towards school work.

We work, and we work hard for six weeks. We try to diligently work on our lessons and projects and attend outside classes for six weeks. Then on the seventh week, all school work ceases. Yes, we literally take a week off of formal school work and lessons. I try really hard to not cram in "catch up" work during our Sabbath Week. Some Sabbath weeks we stay home the entire time and just rest. We continue to read aloud each day. (Missing read aloud time is not an option for me.)

When our family began using our Sabbath Week to truly rest and regroup, our homeschooling radically changed for the better.

Actually, Sabbath Weeks allow more time for extended read aloud time and extra time for independent reading. We sleep in. We cook, we bake, and we play. We play lots of board games. We used to build forts, paint, and get dirty in the yard. Some Sabbath Weeks the weather is beautiful and the great outdoors calls us out to play. Sometimes we schedule extra play dates and outings with friends. We do extra nature studies and go on hikes. We go on a few field trips. I make sure that whatever I schedule during our Sabbath Week it is something truly relaxing. I don't want to spend hours in traffic to have a snow day during our Sabbath Week if the trip, the drive, and extra planning will steal my joy and create added stress. I fell so much in love with this idea of a Sabbath Week, I incorporated it into the classes and co-ops we lead. We instituted Sabbath Weeks in the Wednesday co-op classes we run by rearranging the calendar. Our co-op meets for six weeks and then we take a break every seventh week. The years I led our science nature club, I made sure we did not meet on our family's Sabbath Week.

The idea is to take a week off from the normal busyness of homeschooling, but to not replace it with a different kind of busy. The idea is to follow the Sabbath Principle designed by God. Take a week to rest, to worship, and to appreciate God's handiwork in your life and to see His fingerprints in creation. Take a break. Rest in God' hands. Give the week to God. Rest in the assurance your obedience will be blessed. Your children will not get behind. Sometimes a break will give you an opportunity to step back and perhaps see something from a

Take a break. Rest in God's hands. Give the week to God. Rest in the assurance your family's obedience will be rewarded.

different perspective. When we are in the thick of an issue or a challenge, it is hard to see through the murky mess. Many times during our week off, God has revealed to me a new way to approach a challenging topic with my son or a creative approach to unlocking feelings tucked away inside my daughter's heart. I have found many math, reading, spelling, and writing concepts need a little time to marinate in a child's mind before they can be fully understood and correctly applied. I often found after taking a break from fractions or spelling rules, my son would approach old problems with new eyes (and often a new attitude). The break would allow my daughter to focus on other things for a while. When she would re-engage with a previous challenge, it was no longer a road block but simply a hurdle she had to jump.

Rest - true rest - gives the brain a chance to chew on information, to mull it over, and to make sense of it. It is like that little annoying circle on my lap-top. When my computer is on overload, it is trying to catch up to my typing and frantic internet searching. It just "thinks and thinks and thinks" and the little icon just spins and spins and spins. No progress is made no matter how many times I hit return or the escape key. That annoying little circle just spins and spins and spins. However when I shut down my computer and fully turn it off, I often return to a

"God will keep him in perfect peace whose mind is stayed on Him, because he trusts in God."

Isaiah 26:3

computer screen that is clear, a keyboard that is functioning, and a modem with increased internet speed. Like our computer, sometimes we need to shut off our minds. When we do, it allows for a better reboot when we turn it back on.

So, yes, even the Principle of Sabbath can be applied to your yearly calendar. Not only should you try to incorporate an hour of rest in each day and a day of rest each week, but pray about adding a week of rest every six weeks. When you are planning your year, mark off every seventh week on your calendar and guard these weeks! Trust God will provide what is needed. Rest in God's promises. *"[God] will keep him in perfect peace, whose mind is stayed on [God], because he trusts in [Him]"* (Isaiah 26:3 NKJV). You will have peace about taking a week off to rest and regroup. God will bless the week and redeem the hours. It will allow God's plans for the week to reign supreme since you do not have any official plans designed by you. Take a deep breath. It is going to be ok. Highlight those Sabbath Weeks on your calendar, reserve them for rest, and look forward to your homeschooling world (and schedules) to be rocked!

CHAPTER 4
Sabbath Year: A Year of Rest

Perhaps you think I am a little crazy, and I have now taken this Sabbath Principle a bit too far. Do you really think I am going to actually suggest you take a whole year off from homeschooling? Well, maybe I am. It's actually not such a radical idea. God did institute the Sabbath Year in Leviticus 25. *"The Lord said to Moses at Mount Sinai, speak to the Israelites and say to them: When you enter the land I am going to give you, the land itself must observe a sabbath to the Lord. For six years sow your fields, and for six years prune your vineyards and gather their crops. But in the seventh year the land is to have a year of sabbath rest, a sabbath to the Lord. Do not sow your fields or prune your vineyards. The land is to have a year of rest"* (25: 1-5 NIV). The Israelites were to give the land a rest every seventh year. Not surprisingly, this is actually a sound agricultural practice backed by today's science and agricultural engineers. Today, farmers use a technique called Crop Rotation. It is similar to God's farming plan in that three or more fields are rotated each year so that one field has a year to rest and lie fallow. Rotating the crops or giving one field

39

a rest from sowing increases soil fertility, crop yield, and soil nutrients. It also limits diseases, pests, weeds and pollution. Come to think of it, maybe you do want to let your homeschooling "field" rest and lie fallow for a year if it means it will yield more fruit, and it will get rid of all the "pests" and "weeds"!

Taking a Sabbath Year was not only good for the land, but it was good for the people. It was meant to help the Israelites deepen their faith in the Lord and to help them learn how to trust God for His

"For six years sow your fields and gather your crops. But in the seventh year the land is to have a year of sabbath rest, a sabbath to the Lord."

Leviticus 25: 1-5

provisions. How were the Israelites supposed to survive without reaping or sowing for a whole year? The food for the Israelites, their servants, and livestock were to come from harvesting the sabbatical year's crop. This meant the Israelites reaped the harvest that grew on its own accord in the seventh year. God promised them, *"I will send you such a blessing in the sixth year that the land will yield enough for three years"* (Leviticus 25:20). In other words, the Israelites had no reason to worry. God promised to take care of them - if they would only trust Him to provide. Obeying this command came with much blessing. However, not honoring the Sabbath Year led to discipline and deportation. God's people were led into captivity for many years due to their disobedience and idolatry. We read in 2 Chronicles how important taking a Sabbath Year was to God. When the Israelites were led into captivity, the Bible mentions that *"the land [finally] enjoyed its sabbath rests; all the time of its desolation it rested"*(36:21 NIV). It appears the only way the land had a chance to rest was to remove the stiff-necked people who were occupying it.

God takes this idea of rest very seriously. I am not suggesting God will remove you from your home if you do not take a Sabbath Year from homeschooling, nor am I suggesting you are sinning if you decide not to skip a year of school. I am suggesting we take a serious look at the idea of a Sabbath Year and what that might look like in our homeschooling journey.   I have read articles and heard of homeschooling families who have rented an RV or chartered a boat for a year to travel the US or to explore the world. I also know a few missionary families who take a whole year off of school to participate in year-long mission trips. I am so impressed with those families for taking such a leap of faith.   I only wish I had the

What might the idea of a Sabbath Year look like in your homeschooling journey?

guts, flexibility, and resources to climb in an RV and explore the United States for an entire year with my family.   What a learning experience that would be! Our family never felt called by God to take a whole year to travel, however, He has called us to a few Sabbatical Years in other ways and for other reasons.

When my daughter was younger and my son was just a babe, we took a "sabbatical year" from formal homeschooling. It was a rough pregnancy, and my daughter's asthma was out of control. My son was attacked by almost every obscure and contagious virus he could possibly catch, he never slept, and my migraines were back with a vengeance due to sleep deprivation. We tried to start the new school year in September but by October, my husband and I realized something had to change. Putting my daughter in traditional school was not an option, so we prayed for God to show us what to do. While I waited and begged for answers, I started attending Bible Study Fellowship (BSF) with my daughter on Wednesday mornings and began participating in every field trip our homeschool group offered. Little did I know, God was answering my prayers, and I didn't

During a Sabbatical Year:
1. Read God's Word
2. Read aloud every day.
3. Visit local library every week.
4. Do nature studies.
5. Learn a new skill.
6. Play games.
7. Attend field trips & park days.

even realize it. In hindsight, what I was doing out of desperation was actually God whispering in my ear His plans for our family that year.

During that "sabbatical year," we didn't crack open one textbook or one math workbook. We read God's Word to prepare for our weekly Bible Study class. We visited our local library every week for their story time and to pick up our weekly supply of picture books to read. We started doing nature studies in our backyard, in our local mountains, and on our hikes. My daughter is very creative so we spent hours at the $1 store hoarding supplies for all of our arts and crafts projects. We played tons of card and board games and made up several of our own. My daughter began taking piano lessons and joined a local musical theatre company. And when we could, we participated in field trips to local gardens, zoos, arboretums, outdoor parks, and aquariums. I didn't plan our day's lessons because I didn't have the mental or physical strength to think about it. Looking back, this sabbatical year looked and felt a lot like "unschooling" but for my health and the survival of our homeschool endeavor, I needed to rest from the formal and explore being more flexible.

At this time, the homeschool group we were affiliated with required standardized state testing every April. Needless to say, I was beyond nervous about the results. I personally do not put much stock in standardized scores but my husband insisted on them and my in-laws, my mother, and our homeschool critics did. While it was none of their business, they always asked at the end of each school year how the kids did on these tests. I was dreading this year in particular. I knew we did not do any formal lessons in reading, spelling, math, science, or history. I was shocked by the scores! Not only did God bless our sabbatical year, but He blessed it abundantly. My daughter was in the 99% in all academic areas but spelling, which was always low, but this year it was higher than usual. Our sabbatical year of field trips, art, nature, reading, games, and music was a huge success on many different levels. Academically, it was a success. Our health improved. My migraines subsided, and my son actually took a few naps after a few of our field trips. Looking back, I always talk about this particular year of homeschooling as one of my favorites.

"I will send you such a blessing in the sixth year that the land will yield enough for three years."

Leviticus 25: 20

Many years later God gently forced another sabbatical year into our homeschooling planning. My son was having a particularly challenging year academically. He has always struggled with reading, spelling, and working memory. We later found out he was dyslexic with some visual processing issues. Until he was diagnosed and we were taught coping and learning skills, he struggled with self-image and confidence issues. He always felt stupid and behind in everything. The year he was diagnosed with Dyslexia, I felt God calling us to give Joe a sabbatical year. Every fiber in my body was saying this was the worst possible time to "take a break." He was already "behind." He needed to catch up and to learn all of these new reading strategies and visual techniques to help him read and remember better. We just couldn't afford to take a whole year off. I also knew from experience that my son learns best with short, daily repetitions. If we didn't repeat and review math facts, spelling rules, history dates, and science information every day, he would forget them all, and we would have to start over (literally)!

Not surprisingly, every time I gave God an excuse for not taking a sabbatical year with my son, He would bring someone into my life with a powerful testimony, or He would put something in our path that made it abundantly clear which direction we needed to take. There was no way out of this no matter how much I protested, so on bended knee, we jumped into God's plan for my son. At this time, my son was passionate about two things: baseball and Boy Scouts. With much prayer and God's leading, I decided to use my son's scouting handbook as his "curriculum" that year. Since he was already completing badge work with his dad and with his troop, I just let him loose each day to do whatever he needed to do for whatever badge (or badges) he was working on. If he wanted to learn it, we made a way to do it.

His "sabbatical year" did not include one textbook or one formal lesson, but somehow he learned about astronomy, geology, survival skills, environmental science, American history, geography, geocaching, bird study, American government, money skills, and so much more. Along the way, he learned tons of practical skills such as welding, cooking, woodworking, entrepreneurship, gardening, and car mechanics (Yep- all boy scout badges!) That year, he delved into leadership in his troop since he had more time. He helped plan camping trips, scouting activities, and badge work workshops. We included his love of baseball into his badge work too by completing the collection badge (My son has an extensive baseball card collection and autographed baseball collection), athletics badge, fitness badge, and sports badge. (My son continued to play lots of baseball and joined a few travel ball teams.) This was the year my husband also started taking my son to MLB spring training in Arizona for an annual fun Dad/Son trip. For fun, he learned the history of some of his favorite teams, located the stadiums on our US map, and kept intricate stats of his favorite players and of his own personal baseball season. (I didn't realize how intense sports statistics were until my son started calculating slugger percentages and pitching ERA!)

If our homeschool group planned a field trip that was related to any of his badge work, we attended. God was so faithful that He even orchestrated a few baseball stadium tours that year for field trips! The only traditional two things we did during that "sabbatical year" were morning devotions and read aloud. I found a great sports devotion book called *One Year Sports Devotions for Kids* (2011) by Jesse Florea. Every day we read together, but I made sure the books were baseball related. We read about Jackie Robinson and some of the other baseball greats. We read the Tim Tebow story (which was awesome since he is dyslexic too)! We finally found a book series my son liked called *Baseball Card Adventures* by Dan Gutman. We read nonfiction books about how to hit harder, pitch better, and steal faster. And yes, I even let him play his PS4 MLB *The Show* during "school time" and let him participate in Fantasy Baseball with his youth group leader and friends. Surprisingly, he had to do a lot of reading to pick his dream teams and to learn the tricks of the game. I am convinced his reading improved that year because of these activities.

"I will restore to you the years that the locust have eaten."

Joel 2:25

Again, I had no formal plans each day and my only goal for the year was that somehow the "rest" from the usual grind of reading and math would somehow give him the breather he needed to learn at his own pace. God was faithful each and every day. My son "ate of the crops harvested" in years past. Amazingly, the skills and concepts that eluded him in the past were finally starting to make sense to him. He was able to apply the same skills that led him to tears and tantrums the year before. God was using the "crops" from years past as a way to nourish my son's mind during his sabbatical year. It was amazing to watch, and it goes without saying, this was my son's favorite year of homeschooling! The next year, he was ready, willing, and able to tackle more advanced math, writing, and reading. Not only did he not

It is also important we give ourselves grace when unexpected things happen in our lives that cause us to take an extended break from homeschooling.

get "behind" in math but he actually completed his math so quickly, he began Algebra 1 a few years early. The year of rest was just what he needed.

In the spirit of taking an extended break, it is also important we give ourselves grace when those unexpected things happen in our lives that cause us to take an unplanned, extended break. The Lord commands us in times of trouble, distraction, and tragedy to *"Be still and know that [He is] God"* (Psalm 46:10). It is important to take time to grieve as a family when a loved one leaves us and enters into the presence of God. We need to give ourselves grace to grieve no matter how long that takes. If putting the school books and lessons aside for an extended time to grieve a loss, then be still and know that God is with you. It is important to take time to mend broken hearts when separation or divorce enters the walls of your home. We need to give ourselves grace to mend those broken hearts no matter how long it takes. If simplifying our school calendar and daily life for an extended amount of time to grieve the loss of a

Learning to enjoy learning again might be just what your child (and you) need this next season of homeschooling and taking a sabbatical year might be the way God is calling you to do that.

relationship or to start the process of starting over, then be still and know that God is all you need. It is important to take time to care for a family member who becomes sick or when a elderly relative needs our daily care. We need to give ourselves grace to reprioritize our lives and to get used to the "new normal" no matter how long it takes. If schoolwork becomes doing chores and field trips become running grandpa to the doctor, then be still and know that God will be your strength.

It is extremely important to take time to care for ourselves if depression, postpartum, or something similar invades our lives and minds. We need to give ourselves grace to address the issues that are causing our depression no matter how long it takes. We all go through it; some of us suffer harder and longer than others. Depression and mental illness are not a sign of weak faith or weak character. It is important to call it what it is and to seek help. Ask a homeschooling friend or grandma to teach your child a few days a week. Put your child in some outside classes a few days a week. If you take a break from being your child's primary teacher, be still and know that God will be his teacher and great will be your child's peace. On a more positive note, if you need to take an extended break because there is another bundle of joy added to the family, then give yourself grace to rest and sleep as much as you and the new babe need. In the few moments of stillness, know that God is in the midst of the chaos and sleepless nights as well as in the moments of quiet.

If the world was full of magical wishes and homeschool fairytales, what would your ideal year look like if you did dare to take a year off of formal homeschooling? Think big! Think adventurous! There are no limits! What would you do (or not do)? Use these dreams and ideas as your prayers. Seriously ask God if taking a sabbatical year is part of His plan for you, for your family, or for one of your kids. Perhaps the Lord is placing certain things, places, and people on your heart for a reason. Don't dismiss the idea of taking an extended time to follow your heart, mind, body, and soul. Don't dismiss the idea of giving your child a year to "marinate" in the skills you have been drilling over the years. Sometimes the brain needs time to just chew on new concepts in order to process and fully understand them. Don't dismiss the idea of using a "sabbatical year" to allow your child to pursue his passions. You never know if God places these passions on his heart for future kingdom work. Don't dismiss the idea of taking an extended break to grieve or to get well. Learning to enjoy learning again might be just what your child (and you) need this next season of homeschooling and taking a "sabbatical year" just might be the way God is calling you to do that.

CHAPTER 5

Daily Sabbath: Sabbath Each Day

Coffee. I cannot survive each day without my morning cup of java! I've always been an early riser but after my son was born, I had to get up even earlier in order to indulge in just a bit of peace and quiet before the activity of the day began. Each morning, I carve out a little time for Jesus and coffee. I'm a mess if I don't have a minute each morning to pray, read my Bible, and sip my favorite coffee. I know my day is shot if I wake up late, and I don't take time to sit at Jesus' feet. My favorite sweatshirt has this quote written on it: With Jesus in my heart and coffee in my hand, I am unstoppable. If I miss my coffee date with Jesus in the morning, I need to make sure I carve some time during the day to just sit and be still.

When the kids were little, sometimes I needed to take several little "sabbath breaks" during the day. It was the only way to remain sane. If I couldn't find a minute alone in the house, I blasted worship music as I cooked lunch, or I prayed (and cried) in the car while driving to the grocery store. Many times, I would have to take the little munchkins with me to the local Coffee Bean drive thru. They would sleep in their car seats while I sipped my latte in the car. If I could, I would steal a shower. It is amazing what a hot shower can do for you when there are no little people staring at you or tugging at your jeans. To be alone in the bathroom was like a night at the Ritz Carlton! (Well not exactly, but close enough.)

When the kids were older, I would sneak away to have coffee with a friend, or I would chill in the backyard to read a little. If it was an especially hard day full of complaints and whining, I would cook.

"With a cup of coffee in my hand and Jesus in my heart, I am unstoppable."

While cooking, I would make a point of thanking God for each and every little annoyance for the day. "Thank you, God, for the opportunity to clean up that science disaster. The kids learned today that rubbing toothpaste on the wall can get just about anything off of a wall, including permanent markers. Thank you, God, for the grocery store shenanigans. I learned another lesson on how to swallow my mommy pride. Children are a blessing from the Lord. Thank you for my little blessings. Thank you, Lord, for the dog mess all over the carpet. While on my knees, it reminded me to praise you and to thank you for all your gifts, even the small furry ones."

Sometimes my moment of sabbath didn't come until the kids were nestled in their beds. I needed to turn off the day just for a while, or I would lose my mind. Without feeling guilty, I will confess that not all of my nighttime sabbaths were filled with prayer and meditation. I may have used those golden minutes to binge watch a favorite show or to devour the latest political thriller. I would try not to use those precious sabbath

Make a point each day to include a little bit of a sabbath or break time.

moments to catch up on emails or check the latest news on social media. If I did, those moments of rest would soon turn into restlessness and my much needed relaxation would turn into dangerous comparisons.

Make a point each day to include a little bit of sabbath or break time. If you need to, schedule it into your planner. Make an appointment with God and keep it. Make an appointment with yourself and keep it. Make a date with your hubby or a friend and keep it. Do something you love to do or something you find relaxing even if it is just taking a moment to sip and enjoy a hot cup of coffee.

56

CHAPTER 6
Sabbath Margins: Extra Wiggle Room

Being a Type A person, I felt better prepared for each school year if I planned out each subject for each month. If I knew where we were going, I could plan how to get there in a more organized way. At the beginning of each year, I would look at how many chapters were in the math textbook, divide it by nine months, and figure out how many lessons of math we had to do each week in order to finish the program by the end of the school year. I would do the same with most of the other books and curriculum we were using. I would even look at the list of books I wanted to read aloud as the family and figure out how many books I would have to read each month in order to get through the list. I was prepared for the year, but all I was really doing was setting myself up to fail. Inevitably, my plans caused tremendous amounts of stress. I found myself at the end of each week fretting over "how far we were behind" and what we didn't finish. The following week, I would double the workload, so we could "catch up." This of course then stressed out my kids. By Christmas break, I was a wreck. I would spend the break frantically planning what we needed to do in

57

the second semester to make up lost time, so we could finish school at least by the time their friends in traditional school went on summer break.

I think you see where I am going with this. My plans and my expectations were causing me to stress out. It wasn't the teacher's guide or my husband or homeschooling; it was me! My expectations were the problem. When my family would ask if we could take a day off or do a Disney Ditch Day, my answer was usually "No." We were already behind; how could we afford another day of no school! I cringe when I think about all of the fabulous field trips we didn't attend

Plan each week with margins so there is time the next day to redo a math lesson, to rewrite a paragraph or to finish a project.

because we *had* to stay home to catch up on school work. My husband tells me often that I am my own worst enemy and that my expectations for our homeschool and for myself are way too high. Eventually, I began to listen to him and finally, I began to believe him.

My mind was blown one year when a homeschooling mentor suggested I plan a four-day week instead of a five-day week! I know, right!!? From that day on, our weekly homeschool schedule changed. We homeschooled four days a week and left one day free. I tried not to tie our free day down to a particular day of the week. I was trying to learn how to flex my flexibility muscles, so I left our free day open. This way when a really cool field trip came up, we were free to attend. When a unique class opened up, we had a day free to take it. When a service opportunity presented itself, we were free to help. When my husband had the day off or I desperately needed a day to goof off with the kids, we had a free day to do just that. The four-day week also helped with those sick days. I no longer felt guilty about taking a day off to go to the doctor, and I stopped pushing my kids to finish work while sniffling and coughing. The idea of a four-day week was mind-blowing, and it has made all the difference in our homeschool journey.

In her book, *Teaching from Rest,* Sarah Mackenzie also suggests to plan your days with margins. Again, I was intrigued. Years later, our four-day week was working well, but my tendency to plan every lesson down to the day still plagued me. I found myself trying to squeeze 32 weeks of math lessons into a four-day week! The idea of planning with daily margins was the answer my Type A self needed. Instead of planning the most I could in each school day, I planned what needed to be completed with a list of what we could tackle if we finished early or had some extra time left over. This thinking changed our entire day. Our timetable immediately changed when my mindset changed. We were no longer rushing to finish lessons. I was no longer screaming in frustration when yet another math lesson was not completed.

I had an overall plan for the year in each subject, but I didn't tie myself down to a specific timetable. I only planned a day at a time, and my plans were simple. One math lesson a day was enough, but I left a margin for problems or hiccups. If a skill was too hard, I had time and space to cover it again the next day if needed. Reading one chapter a day in our family read aloud was a must but if we had more time, we kept reading. Writing assignments were broken into small steps so each day felt like a success (and my procrastinator was not rushing anymore to finish a five paragraph essay at the last minute).

Plan a 4-Day Week instead of a 5-Day week. Leave one day free for the unexpected or for those spontaneous opportunities that come your way.

Whatever didn't get finished that day rolled over to the next day. I did not add the incomplete work to the next day's assignments; I made the incomplete work the next day's assignments. Do you see the difference? Instead of compounding the lessons the following day, I planned with margins so there was time the next day or the day after to redo a math lesson, rewrite a paragraph, or finish a project.

You might be thinking, "What about the rest of the work? When do you do science, history, art, and language?" We get it done by using the concept of *Morning Time* or *Basket Time* to make sure we cover all the important subjects. It even allows me to include subjects I rarely get to. You know those subjects! The lessons and activities you "save for later for when you have time." Yes, those subjects! The ones you never have time to get to, but the activities you really want to cover. Thanks to Cindy Rollins and Pam Barnhill, using a morning time basket and a rotating schedule saved my marriage, our homeschooling, and my sanity. Morning Time is the brainchild of Cindy Rollins. For over 25 years, her family started each day gathered around mom reading, singing, discussing, and reciting. Pam Barnhill's podcasts, *Your Morning Basket*, and book, *Better Together* (2018), give simple ways to incorporate the idea of basket time into your morning lessons.

Rotate items in your Morning Time Basket:
- Bible memory verses
- Math Games
- Poetry Reading
- Art Studies
- Nature Studies
- Composer Studies

The possibilities are endless and unique to each family.

Everyone's morning time basket looks different, but the basic concept is the same. Place in the basket the two or three things you want to do every morning with the entire family. When our family was younger, I always placed in our morning time basket our devotional book, a chapter book for reading aloud, a few math games to play, and our worship CD. Every morning, we prayed together, studied God's Word together, worshipped together, read together, and played some fun math games together. When my kids were older, I replaced our devotional book with the Bible, I still had a chapter book to read aloud, some games to play (math, science, history, geography, etc), and

Simple Morning Time Basket:

1. Daily Devotions & Bible
2. Read Aloud Book
3. Three or four other things to rotate.

American Voices: A Collection of Documents, Speeches, Essays, Hymns, Poems, and Short Stories from American History by Ray Notgrass (2007) and *Words Aptly Spoken: American Documents* by Jen Greenbelt (2011). No matter what historical time period we were studying each year, when my teens were in high school, I felt strongly that they needed to have a strong foundation in America's Christian and biblical heritage, our founding fathers, and America's form of government, so I included American studies into our morning basket too.

The extra items you place in your morning time basket are the other subjects and activities you really want to do together but never seem to have time to do. When my family was younger, I also placed in the basket poetry books, art prints for art studies, CDs with composers and their masterpieces, our nature study journals, Bible verse cards for memorization, Mad Libs, and map work. Yes, it sounds like a lot to cover, which is why we used a rotating schedule with the rest of the items in our morning time basket. After we did daily devotions, read aloud, played a math game, and worshipped, I would then pick two or three other things from the basket to do that morning such as Bible memory verse, composer study, and Mad libs. The next day after we did our "must do morning lessons" (which were our daily devotions, read aloud, math game, and worship), I would pick two or three different things from the basket to do such as poetry reading, map work, and art study. Then on the next day after we did our daily devotions, read aloud, math game, and worship, I picked two or three other things from the basket to do that morning. If nature study was the only thing we had not gotten to that week, we would work on our nature study journals and then begin the rotation again. By rotating the subjects and activities I wanted our family to learn, it allowed us time to tackle them all over a course of the school year but at a slower, more enjoyable pace.

When my kiddos were older, the extra items in our morning time basket evolved. We still did Bible memorization, but we memorized longer passages. We still did poetry reading and recitations, but we also included Shakespeare. We still did nature studies, art studies, music history studies, and games as a way to help us learn different topics. But at this age, the board games were more challenging such as *Equate* (math games about equations), *Element-O* (monopoly-type game for the periodic table), *The Plays the Thing* (game about Shakespeare's plays), *Constitution Quest* (game about US government), and *Ten Days in Europe* (strategic geography game). Sometimes the more academic high school subjects were a bit dry and hard to understand, so I tried to find a few games each year at the middle and high school level that taught advanced concepts in the form of a game. And those games always found their way into our morning basket rotation schedule.

Overall, our morning basket time lasted about an hour to an hour and half, depending on the age of the kids, the day of the week, and what subjects were in the rotation. Everyone's basket time will look different because every family has their own set of priorities, passions, and needs. The beauty of morning time is it allows your family to start the day off together and to learn together. It maximizes your time. Rotating items each morning is a great way to make sure you hit all of those subjects that are important to you every couple of

64

days. You will no longer feel guilty about never doing nature journals or playing games or learning about the Bard himself. There is no need to do all of these subjects every day. The mind can't handle it, and your schedule can't accommodate it. There are not enough minutes in the day, so stop trying to fit it all in. Plan with margins, learn together, and use a rotating schedule for the extras. For more information on *Morning (Basket) Time*, I highly recommend you read Cindy Rollins' book and listen to Pam Barnhill's podcasts. My explanation is just an example of what we did. You will be blessed by learning how others have designed their morning time routines.

Give your child (and yourself) time and space to breathe. Praise God if the math lesson goes smoothly or the paper is written perfectly, but give yourself time and the grace to revisit a lesson the next day.

After morning time, your children can then begin working on the other subjects but at their own pace and at their own level. This is when your third grader works on his multiplication facts while your middle schooler does fraction worksheets and your high schooler attempts quadratic equations. After basket time, your second grader is writing about his favorite dog while your older student is working on a research report about narwhals. There is plenty of time for independent work at different grade levels after morning time. However, don't forget to plan with margins. Give your child (and yourself) space to breathe. Praise God if the math lesson goes smoothly and the paper is written perfectly the first time, but give yourself time and grace to revisit a lesson or to do revisions the next day. Trust me, when you start planning your day with less in it, you will be a more joyful mommy. You will also be pleasantly surprised at how much gets accomplished when you give your family and yourself the gift of time.

PART TWO:
SIMPLIFICATION PRINCIPLE

Come to Me, all you who are weary and burdened,

and I will give you rest.

Take My yoke upon you and learn from Me

for I am gentle and humble in heart, and you will find

rest for your souls. For My yoke is easy

and my burden is light.

Luke 10: 28-30 NIV

CHAPTER 7
S.i.m.p.l.i.f.y

The Lord promises rest to those who are weary and burdened.
The only requirement is for believers to take His yoke upon them for
His yoke is easy and His burden is light. In Joanna Weaver's book,
Having a Mary Heart in a Martha World (2000), she shares a story of
a man and his cart and what happens when he takes on more than what
God requires. The story begins with an old man talking with God
about his day. God asked him to take a wagon with three stones to the
top of the mountain. God gave the man
specific instructions and sketched a
map in the sand. The man cheerfully
set off pulling the wagon behind him.
He was excited to do what God called
him to do.

> "Rest in the Lord and wait patiently for Him."
>
> **Psalm 37:7**

As he was going through a
small village, a friend stopped him and
asked him what he was doing. He
explained that he was taking the wagon of rocks to the top of the
mountain. The friend became excited as he explained he was just

thinking about how he was going to get his rock to the top of the mountain, and would the man be willing to take the rock in his wagon since he was going that way. Happily and with a skip in his step, the man with the wagon took the friend's rock and started on his way.

As he went along, more and more friends asked him to take their rocks and stones with him since he was going in that direction.

If your yoke is "chafing," then perhaps you are carrying more than God has asked you to.

Eventually, the wagon grew fuller and fuller. The wagon felt huge and awkward as it lumbered and swayed over the ruts in the road. No longer was the man singing praises. Instead, resentment began to build inside. He was tired and the load was too burdensome. His shoulders were bruised and his countenance was saddened. Frustrated, the man had thoughts of giving up and letting the wagon roll backward.

About that time, God came to his side and asked what the problem was. "Lord, you gave me a job that is too hard for me," the man sobbed. God walked over to the wagon. As God held up a big piece of shale he asked, "What is this?" God tossed it on the ground. The man explained about his friend who asked him to bring it up the mountain. God continued to unload the wagon, removing both light and heavy items until only the three original stones were left in the

70

wagon. "Here are the three stones I asked you to bring to the mountaintop. You do not need to carry the others. I only asked you to carry these three," the Lord graciously said.

Surprised, the man replied, "I don't have to bring all of these things up to the top of the mountain? It seemed like something I should do."

God gently said, "I know you were trying to help, but when you are weighed down with all these cares, you cannot do what I have asked of you. Let the others shoulder their own tasks. Let them do the things I asked them to do." With a smile on his face and a twinkle in his eye, the man began to softly sing a little tune as he joyfully continued his journey. He knew he was doing what God asked of him, no more and no less. His task was truly doable, the Lord's burden was truly light, and His yoke was truly easy.

For me, there have been many seasons when my shoulders were irritated by "my wagon's load." I had figurative bruises on my arms and chafing on my back from the heavy load I was determined to carry. I noticed when I put too many stones in my proverbial wagon, not only was the load too burdensome to carry, but the chafing caused figurative (and sometimes literal) pain and irritation. Like the old man, I would cry out to God, "Why, God, why? This call to homeschool is too hard! I can't do it!" But the Lord would gently remind me His yoke was easy. The reason my yoke was chafing and causing so much pain was because I chose to add things to my homeschooling wagon that God didn't necessarily call me to do.

When we are feeling overwhelmed with too much to do, perhaps it is time to reevaluate our "wagon." Perhaps we need to dump out a few rocks. We need to look at what we're doing and

When the chafing begins and the load becomes too burdensome, it is time to prioritize the "rocks in our cart."

decide if we are carrying unnecessary burdens. What is God calling us to do? What are we telling ourselves we have to do? Sometimes the extra rocks we carry for others become too heavy and too hard to carry. Carrying them for others might be helpful to them, but they may not be our load to carry.

I know this is hard to hear because homeschooling mamas have a heart to serve and help others. Academically, the extra rocks might be awesome, but they may not be what God wants our children to learn in that particular season. When the chafing begins and the load becomes burdensome, it is time to prioritize the "rocks in our cart."

When I share this story at conferences, I like to give it a 2020 update. My cart becomes a minivan. In it, God has asked me to deliver several important packages down the 210 freeway. My journey always starts with the windows rolled down and the worship music blaring. However, my leisurely drive down Route 66 begins to take an ugly turn when I reach into my pocket and pull out my "To Do List." While I am out, I need to stop here and there to pick up a few items and to drop off a few things. With each stop, I get a little more irritated. The windows go up because the traffic is so bad. The music is hardly heard above my complaining. As I look around the minivan, I realize I am doing more carschooling than homeschooling. Books are spewed all over the floor. Food crumbs are nestled in between the seats and the floorboards. The pile of coffee mugs are sticky and dirty. The kids in the backseat are bickering while I firmly whisper through clenched teeth to hush so I can concentrate.

This is where the second Principle of Simplification comes into play. Not only do we need to include the Principle of Sabbath into our family life and homeschooling, but we need to include the idea of simplification. My next door neighbor had a magnet on her refrigerator that was attached to a Matthew 6:33 verse. The magnet said, "Keep it simple, stupid!" When I asked her why the harsh reminder magnet,

PRINCIPLE OF
SIMPLIFICATION:

S: Start with the end in mind.
I: Invite others on the adventure.
M: Mark Twain Philosophy
P: Put the HOME back into HOMEschooling
L: Less is more.
I: Internet: Unplug & Plug In
F: Flexibility is key.
Y: Your ultimate job description

she replied, "All the Lord requires of me is to seek His Kingdom, to seek His righteousness, and to seek His face. God wants my life simple. I keep messing it up by making it complicated." Homeschooling really can be quite simple. Notice I didn't say it would be easy, but I did say it can be simple. God requires us to seek Him in all we do, but we are the ones who make His will for our lives and our family so complicated.

In Part Two, we will explore the *Principle of Simplification* using the acronym S.I.M.P.L.I.F.Y:

S.   Start with the end in mind.

I.   Invite others on the adventure.

M.   Mark Twain's Motto

P.   Put the *Home* back in *Home*schooling.

L.   Less is More.

I.   Internet: Unplug and Plug In.

F.   Flexibility is key.

Y.   Your Ultimate Job Description

The Principle of Simplification is more than just getting back to the basics. It isn't about finding the perfect curriculum or using one methodology over another. Once you truly apply the Principle of Sabbath to your homeschooling lifestyle, you will have the time and energy to finally *just breathe*. You will have the time to sit at Jesus's feet, to seek His plan, and to bask in His goodness. It is when you truly rest you can begin to simplify. Brew yourself another cup of coffee, take a deep breath, and explore on the Principles of Simplification in Part Two.

It is when we
truly rest that
we can begin
to simplify.

CHAPTER 8

S: Start With The End In Mind

In Lewis Carroll's classic, *Alice in Wonderland*, Alice stopped to ask the Cheshire Cat for directions. "Would you tell me, please, which way I ought to go from here?" We can learn much from the Cat's response, "Well, that depends a good deal on where you want to get to!" Surprisingly, Alice told the Cat she didn't really care where she was going. The Cat's response was priceless: "Then it doesn't really matter which way you go, does it?"

The Cheshire Cat summarizes the importance of why we need to start this homeschooling journey with the end mind. If we know where we want our children to end up at the end of their formal education, then it will be easier to plan the journey. The baseball great, Yogi Berra, once said, "If you don't know where you are going, you'll certainly end up someplace else." How true this is! If we don't know what we want our children to know and value at the end of their homeschooling journey, then we are taking a chance on what our children will actually learn (or not learn)!

The first thing every homeschool mom should do before starting to home educate her family is to ask herself the following question: Why do I want to homeschool my child? The answer to this question will dictate every important choice you make, so having a clear understanding of your motives are imperative. What is the main reason you decided to homeschool? I suspect it was a myriad of academic, social, and scheduling reasons: too much homework, sleep deprivation, wasted time, schoolwork not challenging enough, invasive secular worldview agendas, teaching to arbitrary standards, a wasteland of busy work, school safety (or lack thereof), mindless testing practices, inappropriate lectures, and /or array of mind-numbing books and textbooks. However, I know the main reason the majority of us accept the call to homeschool is because we feel God is calling us to it. We long to make God's Word the focal point of our lessons, to use curriculum with a biblical worldview, and to teach values that are in line with our Christian beliefs. In essence, we want to teach and live out Deuteronomy 6:4-9. "*Hear, Israel, and be careful to obey so that it may go well with you and that you may increase greatly in a land flowing with milk and honey, just as the Lord, the God of your ancestors, promised you.*

"If you don't know where you are going, you'll certainly end up someplace else."

-Yogi Berra

Hear, O Israel: The Lord our God, the Lord is one. Love the Lord your God with all your heart and with all your soul and with all your strength. These commandments that I give you today are to be on your hearts. Impress them on your children. Talk about them when you sit at home and when you walk along the road, when you lie down and when you get up. Tie them as symbols on your hands and bind them on your foreheads. Write them on the doorframes of your houses and on your gates."

Before your schedules fill up, curriculum arrives, and autopilot takes over your car, take a moment to remember your calling and why you came home in the first place! God first, then everything else. Family first, then everything else. Home first, then everything else. Pray about ways you can keep God and His Word as the focal point. Spend time in God's Word and on your knees asking God what that might look like for you and your family. I promise you won't regret it (and your children won't mind) that you chose to not only learn together, play together, eat together, but to pray together, to study God's Word together, and to grow in your relationship with Jesus Christ together.

"These commandments I give you today are to be on your hearts. Impress them upon your children."

Deuteronomy 6:8

Before we started homeschooling, my husband and I used our answer to this question to develop our family's *Homeschool Mission Statement*. Our main reason we chose to homeschool was because we felt God was calling us to do so. We wanted the freedom to homeschool so we could integrate God's Word into everything we did and into every subject we learned. We also wanted our familial relationships to be close, which included our two children having a special bond and friendship as well. Finally, we wanted our children to enjoy learning. We didn't want school to be a chore. We didn't want learning to be a bore. We wanted them to embrace the idea of becoming life-long learners. Ultimately, these are the three things my

God first, then everything else!

husband and I desire our children to learn and be able to do when our official homeschooling is complete: *We pray that our children will love the Lord, love each other (and those God puts in their paths), and love learning.* This is our homeschooling mission statement, and it is what I use to guide my planning each and every year. It is our end goal.

When our children graduate high school, we pray they will have the courage, confidence, and curiosity to leave home, but that they will also have the desire and longing to come back home and share with us their experiences, accomplishments, and failures. We want to raise individuals who value God and His Word and who want to share it with those they encounter. We want to raise individuals who value family and respect those they meet (even if they do not agree with them). We want to raise individuals who are independent learners, who are curious enough to ask questions and competent enough to teach themselves and others. We want to create a family environment where memories are made and traditions are cherished. At the end of our homeschool journey, we hope they feel so connected to our family that after they explore and make their mark in the world, they want to come home to tell us all about it.

Why do you want to homeschool?

The answer to that question should dictate every important choice you make.

Why did you choose to homeschool? Use your answer to create your family's *Homeschool Mission Statement*. Write it down. Hang it on your wall so all can see it. Put it in your Bible as a reminder. Visit it each year and revise it when necessary. At the end of twelve plus years, your children will end up somewhere. Make sure it is where you want them to be.

Next, ask yourself this question: In twenty years when your children are asked about homeschooling by co-workers or college roommates, what three words do you hope your children will use to describe their homeschooling experience? While writing this chapter, this was not a particularly good week in the De Francisco home. I may have lost my mind and said a few things I know I should not have said, and I know for a fact, I did a few things I should not have done. If my children were asked that question today, they would probably give these three words: crazy, stressful, and useless. Obviously, these were not the three words I hope my children would use to describe me, our home, or their homeschooling experience.

When I was asked this question many moons ago, my original three words were love, laughter, and literature. My heartfelt desire was for my children to look back on our homeschooling years and smile (and even laugh). I want them to know with every fiber of their being how much they are loved. Looking back, I want them to remember how much we believed in them. I want them to look back and remember that even when they didn't think they could do something or learn something, their dad and I were their biggest and loudest cheerleaders. I want them to remember that even when they failed, we were the first ones there to help them up. Through snuggles during read aloud time, bedtime heart-to-hearts, and academic struggles, I hope they know they are loved and cherished. I want them to think of my crazy laugh (not my hysterical outbursts). I hope they remember our home as a safe and secure place (not a stressful and out of control camp). I want them to look back on all of the lessons we learned together as helpful, exciting, and even fun (not pointless and useless).

Because love was first on my list, I made sure we had lots of family devotions. I made sure I had one-on-one time with each child every day and I made sure I took them out once a week (or once a month) just the two of us. It was my way of sharing with them something they loved. It was a way of checking in with them, which was very important as they got older. Since laughter was also on my list, I made sure we had time to be silly and to play lots of games. I tried not to take myself too seriously (which was never a problem with my son around! My daughter keeps me grounded and my son keeps me humble!) Finally, I made sure we read lots and lots of literature. Reading aloud as a family is one of the best and easiest ways to connect  Create a Family Homeschool Mission Statement.

with your children and to build life long memories. It is a great way to rest, relax, and snuggle together. Reading great books allows for great discussions about faith, values, and issues in the world. Our home was filled with books and our days were filled with read aloud time.

Like your family's Mission Statement, write these three words down and tuck them away. Keep them handy. When you are having "one of those days," pull out your list of three words. Remind yourself why you are doing this. When nothing seems to be going well, then eliminate all of the extra stuff that day and just do the basics. It's ok! You will have plenty of time tomorrow and next week to catch up on everything else. Don't make a bad day worse by plowing through an academic "to do list." I call these my "Back to Basic Days" except my 3 R's are reading, writing, and relaxing. Sometimes, you've just got to do it!

If it is a really bad day, then do only one thing that day. If one of your three words was "read aloud time," then spend the day

On really bad days, eliminate one thing at a time until the chaos calms down.

snuggling and reading. If your one word was "fun," then spend the day playing games. If your one word was "service," then spend the day cleaning, helping a neighbor, or volunteering somewhere. If your one word was "exploring" or "adventure," then spend the day outdoors hiking, planting, or climbing trees. Keep your list handy so when you feel like giving up or giving in, you are reminded of why you are homeschooling and what your end goals are.   Spend the day doing things that break the negativity and help you breathe a little easier.

Once you have your family's Mission Statement written, the most important thing to do before you start homeschooling or you start a new year of homeschooling, is to set aside a *Day of Dedication*.   Each year before planning our homeschool year or purchasing any new supplies,   I spent a whole day on my knees

Before the school year begins, set aside a Day of Dedication to seek God's plan for your school year and to pray over your children.

covering our new school year in prayer. First, if you have little ones, I strongly suggest you get your hubby on board or enlist a fellow homeschooling mom to help. When my kids were younger, I would set one whole day aside in August. My husband would take the kids on a fun, all-day outing so I could have the entire house to myself.

Then, I spread out all of the books, curriculum, class flyers, computer CD's, etc on the family room floor. Each year, I literally get on my knees, bow before my heavenly Father, and pray over everything. I pray that God will meet us each and every day in our lessons and in everything we will study. I pray that my family will meet God in a new way this coming school year and that our knowledge, love, and devotion to Him and His Word would be deepened through all of our studies. (Yes, I even pray God would not only help us get through math without tears but that my kids would see God in a new way through studying even math!) I pray that God's

Choose a verse or biblical promise for each child, then pray this verse each morning as you prepare your lessons.

plans, not my plans, will prevail in the new school year. I pray that His will, not mine, will be done. I pray for the courage to really let God take control of our school year and that I would obediently and cheerfully take the passenger seat. I pray for God to give me discernment on what books, classes, and curriculum are important to my child's growth and development this year and which ones can or should be eliminated. I then pray for the courage to remove the things from our schedules, our lessons, (and maybe even our lives) that are not God's best for each child.

After I pray over our books and our plans, I then dedicate the year and all we do to the Lord. Each year I find a verse I feel God is calling us to obey or a promise to claim. I print the verse several times. I put it on our refrigerator. I put it in my Bible as a bookmark. I write it on the inside of our planners, and I keep it saved on my laptop as one of my screensavers. I write it on our homeschool chalk wall. I find having the verse everywhere reminds me to pray the verse and pray it often!   The Lord always makes it clear to me what our yearly verse should be.

Once the Holy Spirit shows me our family verse for the year, I claim it! I pray the verse over our family and then dedicate our lives, our family, and our school year to the Lord: *"May everything we do and say be for the honor and glory of our Lord, Jesus Christ. May the words of our mouths and the meditations of our heart be acceptable in His sight. May the Lord bless us, keep us and shine his face upon us. May the Lord be gracious to us, turn his face upon us and give us peace"*(1 Corinthians 10: 31, Ps 19:14, and Numbers 6:24-26).   Each year, I also pray Ephesians 3:14-21 and insert each child's name into each verse.

Next, I turn my attention to each child in particular. In prayer, I write four to five goals for each child. One is always a spiritual goal, one is usually a social or emotional goal, one is an academic goal and one goal focuses on character. As my kids matured, I included them in picking a spiritual goal, an extra academic goal, and even a personal growth goal. Even  Make family devotions a priority but keep it simple! when my daughter went off to college, I asked her what specifically she wanted me to pray for her during the academic year. Using these goals, I pray for God to reveal a personal verse for each child. I look through my Bible and my journal for scripture verses that God had been sharing with me during the summer. Sometimes I even include a personal Bible verse I feel God is declaring as a promise for a particular child. Once a verse is revealed, it becomes the child's theme verse for the year. I pray this verse for my child each morning as we prepare for school, and I pray this verse each week as I plan lessons.

Finally, I decide what our family devotions will look like for the year. No two years have been the same. A few years may have been similar but as the kids grew, their personalities developed, their character strengths (and flaws) became apparent, and our family schedules changed, so our morning devotion time also changed. Every season of homeschooling has been different. Therefore, our family devotions were molded to meet our spiritual needs each year. When the kids were young, we simply read a Bible story during family devotion time from either *DK's Illustrated Family Bible* or *The Child's Story Bible* by Catherine Vos. I would switch back and forth between the two Bibles for variety. Each morning, we would simply read a Bible story, discuss what happened, what we could learn from the story, and most importantly, how we could apply those truths that very day!

Some years I would pick a devotional that related to our main topic of study for the year. A few years we focused on animal studies and zoology so we used *God's Amazing Creatures and Me* by Haidle. One year when the kids were older and our science studies focused on zoology again, we used *The Big Book of Animal Devotions* by Coleman. Not only were we learning about God's creation, but we were also connecting it to biblical truths. Several years we "traveled" the world through history, art, science, math, and literature, so we used *Window on the World* by Spraggett for our daily devotional. We used it again in high school the year my son took Comparative Religions. Each page gives a description of a particular culture or country and then gives ways to pray for that country.

Some years we did Bible Study Fellowship (BSF) as a family, so the kids and I read the Bible passages and answered the group discussion questions together. Our favorite BSF studies were The Life of Moses (Exodus to Deuteronomy), Acts of the Apostles (an awesome study of Paul and most of his epistles) and The Gospel of John. As the kids matured, they each read independently either from their Bibles or from a little devotional book. When my son was middle school age, he loved *The One Year Sports Devotional* book. My daughter was always partial to anything related to the study of Esther. Sometimes we would just pick an inspirational book we wanted to read as a family. I would read a chapter during family devotion time and then we would discuss biblical truths and daily applications shared in the book. Some of our best discussions were sparked by Ben Carson's biography,

Gifted Hands, Tim Tebow's book, *Shaken*, and C.S. Lewis' *Screwtape Letters*.

As you are planning your school year, not only is it important to start with the end in mind, but to keep your focus on God and His Word. Will your children succeed academically? Yes! That is a given, so don't worry and fret over that. Your children already have an academic advantage because you chose to homeschool. Will they struggle? Probably in some areas. Will learning be easy for students with learning disabilities? No, but it will be easier with you as their teacher. Keep your focus on why you chose to homeschool.

What's more important?

Heaven or Harvard? Relationships or scholarships?

Character or curriculum?

Progress or perfection?

Perspective should be placed on acceptance into Heaven not Harvard, relationships over scholarships, character over curriculum, and progress over perfection (and this is for mom too)! Remember to start each day and end each day with prayer and to always keep your eyes on Jesus.

CHAPTER 9

I: Invite Others Into the Adventure

In conversations with friends over the years, many have told me they could never homeschool their children. They would say things like "I can't be home alone with my kids all day every day. I would go crazy!" I purposely refer to homeschooling as an adventure and a journey. It can be quite an adventure, and yes, it can also get a little crazy. If you have been called home to educate your own children, welcome to this wild and crazy adventure we call homeschooling! If you have been traveling this road less traveled for a few years now, and God has called you to continue homeschooling, then welcome back to another year of homeschooling adventures.

Like most family trips, those traveling probably have different feelings about the trip. You might be kicking and screaming as you begin your new homeschooling journey, you might be excited about the new possibilities that educating your own at home brings, or you might already be tired just thinking about what you need to "pack" as you prepare for yet another year of lessons. In the past few years, there has been a mass exodus out of the traditional school system as many moms have felt the stirring of the Holy Spirit to come home and homeschool their own. Many of us, who are already homeschooling, continue to hear the calling to stay home and to continue home educating our own. No matter where you are on this homeschooling journey, have no doubt! You were called home for a reason. That reason may be abundantly clear to you, or you may still be struggling to figure out God's master plan for your call to come home. Wherever you find yourself today, rest in the assurance that God has called you home, and He has called you to homeschool.

Why has God called you home to homeschool? Is it to mend a broken relationship? Is it to work on character and heart issues? Is it

Don't do this homeschooling adventure alone. We need to invite others on this homeschooling journey with us.

to build family bonds? Is it to keep God and His Word a priority (or to make it a priority)? Is it to pour into that strong-willed child? Chances are the main reason you were called home to homeschool has very little to do with academics and everything to do with God. Sometimes we don't really fully understand God's call home until much later in the journey. Like the expression says, sometimes it's the journey not the destination that matters.

Don't take this homeschooling journey alone. We need to invite others along this adventure with us. Find a support group you can call your "home away from home"! Is it possible to take this homeschool journey alone? Sure, but it is easier and more fun with others. *"A person standing alone can be attacked and defeated, but two can stand back-to-back and conquer. Three are even better, for a triple-braided cord is not easily broken"* (Ecclesiastes 4:12 NLT). Find like-minded moms who are on this homeschooling adventure to support you, pray for you, and even learn along side you. Finding a community is just as important for your children as it is for you. Sometimes it can feel like it is us against the world. God calls us to fellowship and to do life in a community. Make sure you find the time to make community a priority.

"My word will not return empty, but will accomplish what I desire and achieve the purpose for which I sent it."

Isaiah 55:11

Ask your spouse, grandparents, aunts, uncles, leaders, coaches, and mentors to join you. What are your husband's gifts? Does he love to hike, garden, or build things? Is he good at math or finances? Include him in the planning and then ask him to take charge of at least one area of your homeschooling each year. When the children are younger, perhaps he can read bedtime stories to the family. Maybe one year he can share his love for gardening or hiking and take over science. Perhaps he can give lessons on personal finance and teach math to the older ones. If his job is too demanding, then perhaps he can take the kids out on Saturday mornings for some "Dad time." Is grandma close by? Is she well enough to participate in your children's education? If the in-laws do not approve of your homeschooling decision, then you should definitely ask them to help. The extra time with the grandkids will not only soften their hearts, but they will see the advantages of homeschooling in action. Does grandma have beautiful cursive handwriting? Ask her to teach the children. Can she knit or sew? Perhaps she can come over once a week to work on a sewing or knitting project with them. If she loves to take the kids places, then designate Grandma as the "Director of Fun" and send the kids with her on field trips. You will enjoy the much needed break, the kids will build wonderful memories, and grandma will cherish the extra time with them.

How can you get grandparents, mentors, coaches, and youth group leaders involved in your homeschooling?

Don't forget about coaches and youth group leaders. My son loved going to lunch once a week with his youth pastor and playing Monopoly Go with his youth group leaders. One year, our worship leader taught my son how to play the piano. My daughter still keeps in touch with her youth group leader who took her out to breakfast every Sunday morning before church. Since my daughter spent five days a week, four hours a day at the dance studio, her dance teacher took the opportunity to speak truth into her life during her teenage years. Both of my kids learned photography from a friend of the family who took the time to share his passion with them. On different occasions, he took them on professional photo shoots and then allowed them to help edit the pictures. My son's baseball coach gave him more advice on life, love, and God during hitting lessons than on how to pitch, hit, and steal. Find those mentors and include them on the journey.

Finally and most importantly, don't get caught in the comparison game. Let's face it, mamas! We are experts at comparisons. Not surprisingly, it is hard not to compare. The proverbial Jones do not live next door anymore. They live on our computer screens 24/7 constantly reminding us how we don't match up to their perfect little families, their perfect little homes, and their perfect little school rooms. It is hard not to compare their "perfection" with our crazy little families, messed up kitchens, and incomplete workbooks. We are all guilty of it. In our well-meaning efforts to be the best mom and best teacher we can be, we stop breathing, and we start hyperventilating.

When you invite people into your lives and to come along this homeschooling adventure with you, make sure you are transparent. Share the good, the bad, and the ugly. When you post the super great

"Three are even better, for a triple-braided cord is not easily broken."

Ecclesiastes 4:12

days and awesome handmade projects, don't forget to post the bad days too. Keep it real. Show the world and your friends you are not perfect and that your cute little Einstein isn't perfect either. Ask for advice and be humble enough to take it. Post the ugly too. Is the enemy wreaking havoc in your life? Is the toddler having temper tantrums, the teenager having meltdowns, and mom having a mental breakdown? It is ok to not be perfect for when we are weak, He is strong. It is ok to claim the good, the bad, and the ugly in our lives. You never know who will be blessed by your transparency, humility, and messiness. You can homeschool alone, but it is so much more rewarding for both you and your family if you invite others along for the ride.

CHAPTER 10
M: Mark Twain's Motto

The beloved American satirical author, Mark Twain, is known for many witty quotes about life, love, and politics. My favorite, however, is also part of our Homeschooling Motto: *"Never let schooling get in the way of your education."* The paradox is so simple yet so true! As I'm teaching history or science to my children, I often find myself wondering how I missed so much information when I was in school. I quickly realized very early on in our homeschooling journey that either I didn't pay much attention in school, the school system didn't teach me much, or perhaps it was a little bit of both. I find I am learning more now as a homeschool mom than I ever did as a student in traditional school. The subjects I hated in school, like history and math, are now my favorites as I teach them to my kids. Perhaps I didn't retain much because I was force-fed the information and then required to regurgitate it back. I had no say in what I was learning so I had no stake in it. Connections weren't made and applications weren't given. We only read dry, out-dated textbooks that were filled with useless information.

However if a song comes on the radio from my younger years, I can sing every word (mostly out of tune) and even remember what year it hit the Top 40. I can still quote lines from *The Scarlet Pimpernel* and *A Separate Peace* because they were books I chose to read while in high school not what was assigned for literature class. I can now quote Shakespeare but that is only because my daughter loves all things Shakespeare. I didn't appreciate the Bard until I studied his life and worked alongside my daughter and her friends. I can still rattle off the states and capitals because as a fifth grader I was fascinated with their arbitrary shapes, and I can retrieve biological and genetic terms from the far recesses of my mind while playing Jeopardy because in high school I was mesmerized by the human body's ability to heal itself. I can honestly say the majority of things I know or still remember as an adult are not the things I was taught in a classroom, but the things I learned outside the walls of the school room.

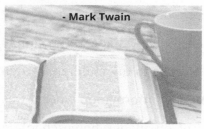

"Never let schooling get in the way of your education."

- Mark Twain

Of course we need to set time aside each day to teach our children what is required by the state. As homeschoolers, we usually stress the academics and even excel beyond what is required. The homeschooler's "problem" usually isn't being mediocre; it is our tendency "to do school" at home. Whether it is fear of the unknown or lack of confidence in our own abilities to teach, we tend to model our home education after traditional schooling. I am guilty of this especially in the first few years of our homeschooling. We tend to teach the way we were taught, so it seems only natural our homes might look like micro versions of a classroom. However, I also find this quite amusing. The reason many of us choose to homeschool is because we see the flaws in the traditional school system. We want better for our kids. We know the school system is doing things incorrectly. Yet when we bring our children home, we model our home schools after the very thing we are trying to escape.

Sometimes we get so caught up in the scope and sequence, the state standards, and the teacher's guides, we let all of that schooling get in the way of our children's true education. If you want to instill in your child a love of learning and whet their appetite for knowledge, then don't model your homeschooling after traditional schools by doing "school at home." Textbooks are fine, and they have their place. Some students learn

Ask yourself:

Why are you modeling your homeschooling after the very thing you are trying to escape?

best with textbooks and many moms breathe easier with checklists. However, I am suggesting that you put just as much emphasis and time

99

into your child's education as you do into his schoolwork. Albert Einstein summed it up this way: *"Education is what remains after one has forgotten what one has learned in school."*

There are facts and then there are skills. There is knowledge and then there is wisdom. There is knowing and then there is doing. Home education is the perfect environment for children to pursue their passions, invest time into their gifts, and explore their interests. It is also the perfect place to learn life skills, volunteer in the community, and help in your family's business. Homeschooling allows more time for creativity, exploring, and independent reading. Research shows it takes less time and energy to learn a new skill when playing. Learning through experience and through play impacts a learner for life.

Don't fall into the trap of doing "school at home."

Early on, it was obvious my daughter loved musical theatre and tap dancing. Because we homeschooled, we had the flexibility and time for her to pursue those passions. Her friends in traditional school also pursued their love of musical theatre and dancing, but they had less time to devote to it. My daughter's schedule was not limited by late night homework sessions because she was able to complete all of her work before lunch, thus leaving her with hours to dance, sing, and rehearse. Later on, she used her passion of musical theatre and singing to earn college scholarships, and she used her tapping skills to start her own business.   The money she earned teaching tap helped pay for her trips abroad and for part of her college tuition.   Because she usually finished all of her school work before her peers, she was also able to assist at her dance studio. Again, she had the time to hone her skill, teach it to others, and make

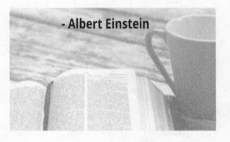

"Education is what remains after one has forgotten what one has learned in school."

- Albert Einstein

money on the side.   In middle school, she also fell in love with baking. Since she had more free time than her peers, she was able to experiment in the kitchen to create dozens of mouth-watering cupcakes, which she turned around and sold every week in our quaint little town.   She used the money earned to pay for more private tap lessons and more cooking supplies.

By pursuing her passions and discovering her gifts, the skills she learned exceeded anything she could have learned completing textbooks. She learned early on how to create invoices for the classes she taught, how to balance checking accounts, how to file tax returns, how to organize her schedules and appointments, and how to invest savings in different ways. She learned how to communicate with adults, peers, her younger (and older) students, write email reminders, and promote her business on social media. She applied chemistry and math skills as she was baking, experimenting, and creating new cupcake flavors and tripling recipes. She honed her research skills as she took master classes, watched countless hours of youtube videos, and read thousands of articles and hundreds of books to become a better performer, dancer, and baker. This also allowed her to learn time management and organizational skills. During her high school years while she was completing a very challenging academic load at the local community college and teaching herself advanced math, she was also getting an invaluable education outside the classroom. Don't let school get in the way of your child's education. Make sure you allow time for your children to pursue their passions. You never know when or how God will use the passions He has placed in their hearts.

By pursuing their passions and discovering their gifts, homeschoolers learn skills that far exceed anything they could have learned by completing traditional textbooks.

My daughter is an avid baker but my son loves to cook! Because the family is home all day together, there are more meals to cook and more mouths to feed. Many homeschool moms use this opportunity to teach their kids life skills like cooking (and cleaning). Take the time to teach your kiddos how to make sandwiches, boil pasta, steam rice, and grill some cheese sandwiches. Assign each child a day of the week to be responsible for preparing and cooking a meal for the rest of the family. Even younger students can be taught how to put together a PB & J sandwich. If you can let go of some control, and you can learn to deal with the mess, eventually, your children will learn how to prepare and cook nutritious and delicious meals for others. For a long time, we just knew that if it was my son's day to cook lunch for everyone, it was going to be scrambled eggs and toast. He didn't vary it much but who cares. It was one less meal I had to prepare. Eventually, his scrambled eggs turned into gourmet omelets with a side of homemade hash browns. During my son's eighth grade year, he took a class with a local chef, learned knife skills, cutting skills, the chemistry behind gravies and sauces, and the basics of different ethnic dishes. Teaching your children to cook and investing in the time to make it part of their education will pay off in the long run. It will bless you in the future and your future daughter-in-law will thank you!

In the classic homeschool book by Dr. Raymond Moore, *The Successful Homeschool Family Handbook* (1994), Moore discusses the importance of developing a work ethic in your children. He emphasized the importance of allowing your child to work in the

103

family business and if possible to create his or her own business. With so much free time to create and work, homeschoolers are known for their entrepreneurial spirit and excellence. If you are a small business owner, then get your family involved. As your children get older, they can begin to help with invoices, bank accounts, promotions, etc. If you or your husband work for someone else, consider teaching your child the skills you use each and every day to make a living. Encourage them to start a side business, to volunteer, to intern, or to work at the local coffee shop.

Allow time for your child to pursue his passions. You never know when or how God will use them for kingdom work.

Our family runs a co-op for homeschoolers. We meet once a week, and we offer classes for Pre K-12th graders in all subjects and extra curricular. We encouraged our kids to get involved in the family ministry even when they were young. When my son was younger, he loved to spend hours and hours building with Legos. Mini figures were his favorite. He collected so many boxes of mini figure pieces, he decided to sell some of them. He developed his first "company" called "Joe's Boys." With my help, he designed his own business cards and flyers and used some of his savings to print them. In separate containers, he organized the different mini figure parts. One container had hundreds of top pieces, a second container had a variety of body pieces, another container held the body bottoms, and the final container was filled with accessories like helmets, light sabers, and tools. His flyers and posters read, "Mix and Match" & "Create your own mini figure!" He charged $2 for one complete mini figure or three complete mini figures for $5. He set up his posters and boxes at our local homeschool co-op each week. He came home every week with a pocket full of quarters, singles, and five dollar bills! When he was a junior in high school, he then created and taught a Lego building class at our weekly co-op classes. Kindergarten through eighth grade students signed up each month to build with Joe. He had fun games for them to play, challenging projects to build, and exciting contests to do. My son took what he loved and took part in our family ministry to create his own little "business." Like my daughter, my son certainly didn't let his schooling get in the way of his education.

For me, the best part of learning in a homeschool environment is taking advantage of learning through field trips and games. If I can find a game that fits with a topic we are learning, a math skill that is eluding one of my kids, or a subject we just never have time to get to, I try to find a game for it. I buy it, borrow it, or make it! Yes, I admit it. I am a game-a-holic! And I am proud to say through my example, my daughter is a game-a-holic too! When our family started a new unit, we played a game to introduce the topic. When we needed help remembering information, we played a game. When we were overwhelmed and overworked, we played games. When I needed a break (or the kids needed a break), we played games. While in the car, we played games. While on vacation, we played games. While waiting at the doctor's office, we played games. When math facts were

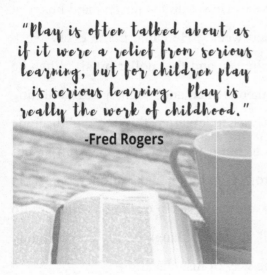

"Play is often talked about as if it were a relief from serious learning, but for children play is serious learning. Play is really the work of childhood."

-Fred Rogers

killing us, we played games. When biology and chemistry terms baffled us, we played games. During election season, we played electoral college games. During the world series season, we played Bible baseball games. Before and after historical field trips, we played games. I think you get the picture. Any time I could use game time as an excuse to put the textbooks away, I did.

Did you know it takes 400 repetitions to create a new synapse in the brain unless it is done through play? If a child is learning through play or games, then it only takes ten to twenty repetitions! So you see, science backs me up too. Playing is our brain's favorite way to learn. Playing games is a great way to learn, review, and reinforce concepts, skills, and facts. It is scientifically proven! There is so little time and so many games to play! Don't be afraid to incorporate game time into your school day.   There is no need to feel guilty about playing *Monopoly, Clue, Guess Who, Chess, Apples to Apples*, or *Scrabble* during school time. The classics are great, and there are tons of new games on the market for just about every subject too. Since we didn't buy a boxed curriculum for our science and history studies each year, I used some of the money saved to purchase one or two new games a year.   After twenty plus years, we have quite an extensive collection of games.   Playing games is definitely a creative way to learn "outside the classroom."

We also used the money saved to go on some great field trips and to invest in an annual pass to a local museum, zoo, or arboretum. Like games, if there was a monument, tour, or museum we could visit to experience a particular time in history, we tried to visit it. The majority of our science "curriculum" consisted of field trips to parks, gardens, observatories, natural history museums, zoos, and aquariums. If we could learn about a particular animal, habitat, or scientific principle up close and personal, we did it. Since

It takes approximately 400 repetitions to create a new synapse in the brain, unless it is done through play, in which case it takes only 10-20 repetitions.

107

we planned four-day weeks with margins, we usually had time to take advantage of field trips being offered by our homeschool group or to explore some fabulous places on our own.

We also planned our family vacations around things we were learning that year. When we studied American History, we spent several weeks in Boston and Virginia learning about the thirteen original colonies, the pilgrims, and the American Revolutionary War. The year we focused on American Government, we spent a week in Washington D.C touring just about everything we could. One year we focused on marine biology and oceanography in science, so we planned many adventures in and around the sea on our family trip to Hawaii. While visiting family in New Orleans, we explored the Battle of New Orleans, plantations, life on the Mississippi, and Civil War battlefields. My daughter delved deep into British history when she traveled to Great Britain her sophomore year and reviewed all she learned about Greek mythology and Ancient History when she traveled to Greece her senior year. If we were able to afford a family vacation that year, my husband and I coordinated where we went and what we did based on what the kids and I were learning in school. It only made sense to make our family vacation into one super long and fun field

Planning a 4-Day week with margins allows time for field trips.

trip.   History, science, literature, art, and music come alive when experienced.   Promise yourself and your family that you will not let their schooling get in the way of their education.

"The recipe for genius: More of family and less of school, more of parents and less of peers, more creative freedom and less formal lessons."

-Dr. Raymond Moore

110

CHAPTER 11

P: Put the Home Back into Homeschooling

What does homeschooling look like to you and your family? It seems in the past few years the term "homeschooling" has been hijacked. Today's homeschooling doesn't look much like the "vintage homeschooling" of yesteryears. In the age of the internet, homeschool conventions, and abundant homeschool curriculum and co-op classes, it is tempting and super easy to do more of your homeschooling outside of the home or online virtually. Don't get me wrong! We are blessed with much freedom and flexibility in today's homeschool culture. However, we may find the freedom of homeschooling a paradox. With so much freedom and flexibility, we can quickly and easily become slaves to it.

What do I mean? Well, with so many wonderful curricula, classes, and co-ops to choose from, you may find yourself doing them all! Is that a bad thing? No, not really. But can it steal your time, your freedom, your flexibility, your joy, and your pocketbook? Most definitely yes! We might find ourselves so busy participating in all of

111

the wonderful educational opportunities available to us, that we are never really home to actually homeschool together as a family.

"Vintage" homeschooling (Charlotte Mason verbiage) or "OG" homeschooling (iGeneration terminology) looked very different to what homeschooling is morphing into today. It is quite ironic that opponents of homeschooling criticize homeschoolers for not being out in the real world, for not learning how to "socialize," and for not learning alongside their peers when in actuality, today's typical homeschooler is hardly ever home! My neighbor used to joke with me

With so much freedom and flexibility, we can quickly and easily become slaves to it.

every time the kids and I packed ourselves and our stuff into the car. "Where are you off to today? Are you sure you homeschool because you guys are never home!" How true this is for many homeschoolers today. And yes, because of this phenomenon, carschooling has become a thing.

My prayer for you is that you will be intentional about putting the *home* back into your *home*school. You don't need all of the extra bells and whistles. You don't need all of the extra funds and all the fancy classes. You don't need all of the approved and accredited classes. It is absolutely ok to learn science and/or history together as a family. It worked long ago for Laura Ingall Wilder and it worked for the pioneers of homeschooling; it will work for your family too. Don't feel guilty that you are reading your way through history or that your older daughter is doing the same physical science experiment (or exploding mess) as her younger siblings, or that your morning hike was also your science lesson for everyone that day. You have permission to stay home as often as you want in order to learn together at home and as a family, and you also have permission to take advantage of as many field trips as your heart desires (and pocket book will allow).

Don't pack your days with so many activities and outside classes that you never have time to enjoy the freedom of being home with your children.

It is perfectly fine to take a break one day (or even a whole week) from endless math workbook pages to spend the day playing number and strategy games instead.

It's not only permissible but highly recommended and much needed that you follow God's plans (not yours) for your day and for your teaching. He called you home for a reason, so He will provide the wisdom, strength, and perseverance to get you through it. And don't forget to have some fun together and to get a little silly! If you are new to homeschooling, my challenge to you is to not pack your days with so many activities and outside classes, that you never have time to enjoy the freedom of being *home* with your kids. In the next chapter, we will explore how you can do less in order to learn more, which will eventually free up more time so you can put the *home* back into *home*schooling.

CHAPTER 12

L: Less is More

When Abe Lincoln was asked how he learned so much without a formal education, he replied, "All I learned, I learned from books." Over the years, overwhelmed moms have asked me, "How do you know you are doing enough?" In our modern society, culture has trained us to believe that the more we do and the busier we are, the more successful we must be. So my usual response to their heart-felt question stuns them and oftentimes causes them to shake their heads in disbelief. I tell them, "Honey, if all your family did today was read from THE good book, the Bible, and read aloud from A good book, then you had a GOOD day!"

If as a family, you read from God's Word, learned some important truths, and discussed how to apply those truths to your daily walk, your day is off to a great start! If your family also has the chance to read a good book and engage in a conversation about the lessons learned, values taught, and how you can use the new insights during the week, then you are having a really good day. I am also positive that while you were reading, other important or interesting geographical, cultural, historical, scientific, artistic, and/or musical concepts were learned too. President Lincoln also stated, "I believe the Bible is the best gift God has ever given man," and President Theodore Roosevelt agreed saying, "A through knowledge of the Bible is worth more than a college education." Don't get me wrong, math and writing are important too, but in the grand scheme of things, I agree with Mr. Lincoln. Just about everything you need to learn can be learned from reading a good book and from reading the Bible.

If you really want to simplify your homeschool and your family life, then stop believing more is better. Change your thinking to *Less is more and simple is better.* This paradox changed my life, my expectations, and my attitude. Think about it. Why did you decide to homeschool in the first place? Chances are you did not agree with what was happening or what was being taught within the walls of the traditional brick and mortar classroom down the street. Yet many moms who bring their children home often model their homeschooling curriculum, routine, and schedules after the very model they disagreed with in the first place. Many new homeschooling

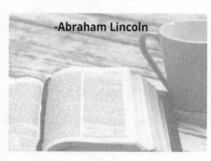

"All I learned, I learned from books."

-Abraham Lincoln

moms try to "do school at home" instead of "home educating" their own. There is a huge difference between the two. True homeschooling comes with freedom and flexibility. It allows a family to educate their children in a way that meets their needs and fits their schedule. No two homeschooling families are alike, so my way of homeschooling will be and should be different than the way you homeschool.

Less is more and simple is always better.

We can learn a lot from other homeschooling moms and why reinvent the wheel if we don't have to, but you should never feel like your kids will only be successful if you homeschool like your friend down the street or if you use a state approved curriculum.

After many years of being on the homeschool crazy train, I have learned the importance of keeping it simple. However, it took me a while to learn these important lessons. At the beginning of each school year, my plans for the year and for each child are usually uncomplicated. I list out the main academic subjects we need to cover along with the books, curriculum, or activities I would like them to do to meet those goals. Then it never fails. My simple plans slowly and innocently become very complicated. This is how it usually happens.

At our first park day, I hear another mom talk about how much she loves their new geography curriculum. The next thing I know, I am asking the mom if I can borrow it and try it out with my family. I then add formal geography lessons to our school day. A few weeks later, my daughter becomes frustrated with something in math, so I begin my usual frantic search on the internet for better ways to teach fractions. Several hours later and a few hundred dollars shorter, my Amazon cart is full and Prime is shipping all of my new fraction games, books, and workbooks to my doorstep. More math lessons are added to our daily school plans. Then, my co-op leader will suggest we look into these fabulous hands-on science classes being offered nearby. When I find out most of my son's friends are already in the classes, I sign up both kids to participate. Extra science classes are now added to our list of things to do.

You had a good homeschooling day if you at least read together from THE Good Book and read together from A good book.

After Christmas, my mother will mention something about my daughter and my son's handwriting. My reaction is to panic, so in January I add learning and relearning cursive writing into our list of things to do each day. By the time February rolls around, our daily schedule is on overload and I am a hot mess. I am stressed out and burned out. We had so much to do and only one semester left to do it in. Before I realized it, I had taken a very simple yet complete set of academic plans and turned them into one big, complicated (and unnecessary) mess. No wonder my children were exhausted, I was frustrated, and my husband was confused. We were going in five thousand different directions because I kept adding more and more stuff to learn and do.

I finally had to change my way of thinking. More is not better! It is quite the opposite. In actuality, less is more and simple is always better. I had to truly try this new perspective out and see if it was true. I committed myself and my family to one year of only doing morning devotions, family read aloud, daily math activities, nature walks, and music lessons. For one year, we stripped away all of the boxed curriculum, outside academic classes, and state standards. I asked the kids what they wanted to learn that year, what they wanted to do as a family, and what they wanted to do in their free time. I don't know why their answers surprised and captivated me but they did. Their ideas and ambitions far exceeded mine. They included things I would never have dreamt of adding or even attempting. Their expectations of themselves and of our homeschooling were far better than mine. After much prayer, chewing on my husband's suggestions, and listening to my kid's input, my list of supplies for that year included just a few things. We dusted off my favorite children's Bible, laminated our library cards, purchased a few simple math workbooks from Costco, found a few journaling notebooks, created a list of free days at our local museums, invested in a new pair walking shoes for all of us, put the tub of Legos in a prominent spot, and collected a bunch of arts and crafts materials from the Dollar Store.

That year, we started each day with our "Soul Food" time, which included breakfast and daily devotions. I told the kids I was feeding their hearts, minds, and tummies all at the same time. Then the kids went off to create. My daughter got busy with the arts and crafts supplies, and my son dove into the containers of Legos. My daughter needed to create before concentrating on math, and my son needed time to get his wiggles out before working on his reading. Our academic time started with reading aloud from either a chapter book, historical fiction, or biography and then we spent time playing a few fun math games. I think I might have played Dogopoly and Sequence Dice five thousand times that year. (This is a hyperbole but not by much!) After that, my daughter did a few pages in her Costco math workbook while my son played outside. Depending on the day, we would do some nature, music, or art studies. Some days, we would go for a walk and attempt to do some nature studies, or we would visit a museum. On other days, we would listen to the life of a composer and draw while listening to his music, or we would read about an artist, look at his/her work, and then try to draw something similar. Then we would spend the rest of the day in unstructured play time. We would spend it outside exploring, hanging out with friends, reading quietly in our rooms, or cooking in the kitchen. Since we had so much free time, my children had time in the afternoon for dance classes, music lessons, theatre rehearsals, and baseball practices. We weren't rushed or hurried. Ironically, they wrote more that year than the years we had a formal writing program. My daughter loved to write in her journal and to create lists. My son was always writing some kind of business plan for the next way he was going to make money. They always had "Thank You" notes to write, invitations to create, and birthday cards to make. I learned that year that less really was more and that simple was really easier. We had more fun that year, and we enjoyed one another's company even more.

During the wonder years (K-5th grade), students learning at home really don't need complicated curriculums and overwhelming programs. If you have found something that works for you and your family, then continue using it until you find it

During the wonder years (K-5th), students learning at home don't need to use complicated curriculums or overwhelming programs.

doesn't work anymore. But for those of you who are tired, overwhelmed, and overworked, try planning less instead of more. Always plan to start your day with morning devotions. If nothing else gets done that day because the baby is screaming, the dog is vomiting, the toilet is overflowing, or math is frustrating, it's ok. God promises,

"Seek first the kingdom of God, and all of these things will be added."
A formal reading program is not really necessary during the early years. Read aloud to your youngsters. As you read to them, they will learn to appreciate good stories, powerful vocabulary, and intricate patterns in the English language. When they are curious about letters and words, then play some fun word and spelling games. Use your library card. It's really the only reading program you need during the wonder years. Fill your home with shelves and baskets full of books. Reading aloud truly is the best reading program.

On a personal note, you may have a child who struggles to read no matter what you do and no matter how much time you give him. If

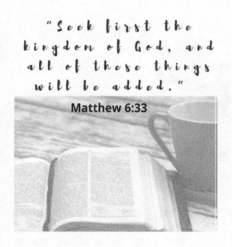

"Seek first the kingdom of God, and all of these things will be added."

Matthew 6:33

this is the case, he may have some sort of reading issue that may need to be addressed. But dear friend, have heart! Home with you is the best place for him. There is no other teacher who understands him better or who wants him to succeed as much as you. There is no other tutor who loves him the way you do and who has been hand-picked by God, his Creator, to be his mom, advocate, and teacher. One-on-one instruction with you is far better than any special class or expensive program offered in the traditional school setting. Outside help might be needed to jump start some new habits, but any challenges your child has, our God can handle. I also highly recommend you read *Better Late Than Early* by Dr. Raymond Moore. The push in modern culture to early reading fluency is not necessary and in some situations can be damaging. Perhaps your child has some processing issues that need to be addressed or perhaps he's just not quite ready to read on his own.

During the wonder years, simplify your writing program too. The best writing curriculum is reading and discussing good books. The best writers are avid readers. When the kids are young, ask them to tell you about the book or chapter they are reading. Engage in conversations about books and about the characters and their choices. Ask open-ended questions like "If you wrote the book, how would you end the story? If you could write a sequel, what would you include? If you could be like anyone in the book, who would it be, or if you could visit anywhere mentioned in the story, where would it be?" By asking these kinds of questions, you are encouraging your child to begin brainstorming and organizing their own original stories.

When your child has an idea for a story (real or silly), ask her to tell you the story or to narrate it to you. Narration is actually her first draft. It may not be written on paper yet, but it is still the beginnings of a plot line for an original story. When she is older or if she thinks faster than she can write or you can type, then encourage her to dictate her story into the computer. It is amazing what Siri can do these days. As a family, write in journals each day. Find a website or a book that includes age appropriate writing prompts. Each day or once a week, read a writing prompt and have everyone (including yourself) write for a few minutes. Younger ones can draw their ideas. Then go around the table and let everyone share their musings. I often found my son, who hates to write, would write pages and pages when I gave him a simple idea to write about and if I also wrote my stories right alongside him. He couldn't wait to hear my thoughts too.

The best writing curriculum is reading and discussing good books. Students learn the nuances of the English language by reading good books.

Add word and spelling games. Incorporate copy work into your Bible memorization. Memorize and write out favorite Bible verses, famous quotes, and inspirational maxims. Find a reason each week to write a card or letter. Grandmas love getting thank you cards, friends love getting homemade birthday cards, and relatives love getting handwritten letters. Writing in the younger years does not have to be formal paragraphs and research papers. Don't feel pressured to make your child write perfect paragraphs every week. There is time for more formal writing programs when they are in middle and high school.

Less is more can be applied to math during the wonder years too. Many math curriculums model their scope and sequence according to national and state standards. While these are great guides, they usually set overly ambitious expectations. When it comes to mathematical skills and concepts that are necessary to learn during the K-7th grade years, textbooks and publishing companies tend to over emphasis the wrong things. Although it may seem like I am oversimplifying what needs to be learned at each grade level, teaching math during the wonder years really isn't rocket science. If you have ever really studied a traditional math textbook, you will notice the repetition. Since math is about mastery, consider digging deep each year into one or two mathematical concepts and skills so your student really

Simple Writing Strategies:

1. Read aloud
2. Narrate and dictate
3. Copy work
4. Journal Writing
5. Word and spelling games

understands them and can apply them well. Moving too fast will only cause much confusion in the middle grades and then feelings of failure in high school.

There is no need to complicate your math time with expensive (and boring) textbooks. My own children didn't use a formal math program until fifth and sixth grade. We used colorful, simple, and inexpensive math workbooks purchased from Costco or an office supply store. When your child is in Kindergarten, they should focus on recognizing numbers and shapes and being able to count. Connecting abstract symbols (0, 1, 2, 3, …52, etc) to an actual number value is quite an advanced skill, so spend time counting with real objects. Give them real opportunities to use numbers. Practice writing numbers and connecting them to what it represents. Look for shapes in your home, in your neighborhood, and on signs. Build with blocks so they also build their spatial problem solving skills. That's it! In Kindergarten, count, cook, measure, play games, and read lots of picture books about numbers.

When your child is in first and second grade, concentrate on learning and mastering addition and subtraction. Teach them these skills together since subtraction is just the inverse of addition. If your child understands 3 + 5 will always equal 8, then when she is asked what is 8-5, she will instinctively know it is always 3. Try to use real world applications for addition and subtraction as much as you can. "If you want that pack of cards, it is $5. You have $8. How much will you have left if you decide to spend your money? Are you ok with that choice?" Use real money and coins as often as you can. Kids learn how to add multi-digit numbers much faster when it is related to money! They also understand regrouping (or borrowing for you old timers like me) much better when subtracting real money. Besides it is a real skill they need to master as adults so why not make it part of your math curriculum from the beginning.

Try to memorize those pesky addition and subtraction facts but try to do it with games, songs, and catchy mnemonics. Some days do a few pages in a colorful addition or subtraction workbook or print up free worksheets from the internet. On other days, play some fun math games. One day a week, set up a make believe restaurant. Have your child create the menu and assign the prices. He can go around taking everyone's order, adding up the bill, collecting money (real or fake), and giving change. My kids loved doing this, and I loved all of the writing, reading, and math they were doing in the process. One week they would set up a pizza pub, another week they would create an ice cream shop, and sometimes they took orders from their "taco truck." Spend first and second grade really learning, understanding, and mastering adding and subtracting whole numbers and decimals (money

Math Skills for Each Grade:

1st & 2nd: + & −
3rd & 4th: × & ÷
5th & 6th: %, % & Decimals
7th & 8th: simple equations, order of operations, & integers

notation). Don't be afraid to add and subtract really big numbers too. Trust me, they can handle it. Again, that's it! In first and second grade, add, subtract, cook, measure, play games, and read lots of picture books about adding and subtracting. *The Pigs Will Be Pigs* picture book series by Amy Axelrod are some of our favorite math picture books.

Once your child enters third and fourth grade, all you really need to focus on is multiplication and division. Again, don't teach multiplication without division since they are the inverse of each other. Like addition facts, multiplication and division sets always go together. Help them see that 3 groups of 5 (3 x 5) is always 15. So if fifteen cookies are shared between five friends, then each friend will get three cookies (because 15 divided by 5 is always 3). The sooner they understand this relationship, the faster they will learn their facts (and remember them).

Like addition and subtraction, try to use real world applications with multiplication and division. Encourage your child to start his own business. Sell lemonade. Make scarves. Bake cupcakes. Walk the neighborhood dogs. When starting their own business, they will quickly see the need for computational skills. "Sammy, if you sell each cup of lemonade for 50 cents, how many do you need to sell to reach your goal of $10?" Include comparative shopping in your multiplication and division scope and sequence too. Have your child help you figure out which sale price is the better deal while shopping. In third and fourth grade, immerse your student in all things related to multiplication and division, which also includes perimeter, area, and volume. When figuring out perimeter, students are simply adding all of the sides together. When figuring out the area of a shape, students are simply multiplying length times width. When calculating volume, students are multiplying three dimensions (L x W x H). Besides, perimeter, area, and volume are real world applications so it will help them see the usefulness of computation skills, especially operations using multiplication and division.

Attempt to teach your fourth grader long division but don't fret if he doesn't master it. In today's technological age, long division is easier done with a calculator. (Admit it! You grab a calculator when you need to divide large numbers or you just estimate.) Once again, that's it! In third and fourth grade, multiply, divide, cook, double recipes, play games, start a business, and read lots of picture books about multiplication and division. Some of our favorite math picture books are written by Marilyn Burns.

Don't ruin your relationship with your child over long division. Don't view a break down or frustration as an interruption. Maybe it is God's new plan for your day.

Yes, even when your child is in fifth or even sixth grade, you still do not need a formal math program. You can still keep it simple. In fifth and sixth grade, spend these two years mastering fractions, decimals and percents. If we are honest, these are three math skills we use almost on a daily basis. We use them when cooking, when shopping, when banking, when investing, when saving, and when paying bills. They are also the foundation of algebraic reasoning. If a student doesn't understand how to add one-half to two-thirds, how will he ever understand how to add a negative 1/2 to a negative 2/3? You are not wasting your time by devoting as much time that is needed to truly understand fractions, decimals and percents and making sure your child can successfully compute with them.

Like everything else, try to use as many real world applications as possible when adding fractions, using decimals, and applying percentages. When you were in school, how many times did you ask your math teacher, "When will I ever use this?" Your student won't see math as useless if he is encouraged to apply it in everyday situations. While in fifth and sixth grade, help your student understand fraction place value and fractional notation. Many students do not understand thirds, fourths and eighths. The symbols 1/3, 1/4 and 1/8 can be very confusing. However if you tell your child he can only have *one* slice of pizza but he can choose if the pizza is cut into thirds, fourths, and eighths, he will quickly realize thirds is the way to go!

130

One slice of pizza out of three is much bigger than one slice of pizza out of eight.

Instead of investing in an expensive math curriculum in fifth and sixth grade, use the budgeted money to purchase manipulatives that will help teach your student to visualize fractions and decimals. A box of base ten blocks and real money are by far the best ways to teach decimal place value and computation skills. My favorite fraction manipulatives are fraction circles, pattern blocks, and Cuisenaire Rods®. They help students visualize fractions in multiple ways. One half is always a half, right? Well, it depends on the unit being cut in half. Would you rather have half of a dollar or half of hundred dollars? Would you rather have half of a cupcake or half of a sheet cake? It's all relative! Using different manipulatives of varying shapes and sizes will help students ask critical questions and apply good problem solving skills with relation to fractions, decimals, and percents.

Help your student master adding, subtracting, multiplying, dividing, comparing, and ordering fractions as well as decimals. I'm sure your daughter or son has asked this question out of frustration many times: "Why do I need to find common denominators when adding or subtracting fractions?" If you are adding two apples and three oranges, what is the answer? You have five pieces of fruit. The answer can only be given using the common denominator between apples and oranges. The common denominator is that they are both pieces of fruit. The same is true for fractions. When your son truly understands fractions and decimals, he will not be confused when multiplying fractions and he sees his answer is smaller than what he started with. For example, what's half of a half (or 1/2 x 1/2)? Your son may have memorized the procedure for multiplying fractions, but he may not understand why it works and why the answer is less than what he started with. Use your leftover pizza from last night to help him understand. Let's say you have half of a pizza left over. Tell your son he can have half of it for lunch today. Isn't his portion smaller than what he started with? That's because if you start with a half of a pizza and you half it again, you will end up with something smaller. That is why when you multiply fractions your answer is smaller. When eating half of the half of pizza left over, he is actually eating one-fourth of the original pizza.

Spend these two years exploring fractions, decimals, and percents and understanding why the computation procedures work. This way when they forget the steps, they can at least mentally estimate a reasonable answer based on their fractional number sense. When learning fractions, decimals, and percents, you still do not need fancy curricula. All you really need to do is cook, halve recipes, work with money, play fractional games, experiment with manipulatives, and read lots of picture books about fractions and decimals. You will be amazed at how many there are at your local library! My favorites are *The Hershey Fraction Book*, *Fraction Fun*, and *M & M Math*. There is something about food and money that help students really understand and appreciate fractions and decimals.

Once your student is middle school age, then a formal math curriculum is helpful. When your student is in seventh and eighth grade focus on those pre-algebraic skills like positive and negative numbers, simple equations with variables, geometry formulas, exponents, and order of operations. Daily practice is necessary, but don't feel like your student has to do every problem on every page. Remember, less is more. If he can successfully find the area of a circle and the volume of geometric cones fifteen times, he probably can do it another 25 times. At this stage of the game, doing math every day is helpful. Skills build on each other and can quickly get complicated so use your freedom of homeschooling to go at your student's pace. Spend more time on equations if he needs it but skip the chapter on absolute value if he mastered it in one day.

Incorporate calculators at this stage (if you haven't already). In this day and age, it is just as important that your student can correctly use a calculator as it is to make correct change. The calculator is only as smart as the person who is punching in the numbers. The calculator will also help the student who never quite mastered his multiplication facts. When using a calculator in high school, he can focus more on the complicated processes while letting the calculator do the simple stuff. Still try to incorporate as many real life applications when learning pre-algebra skills. Students understand positive and negative numbers more when in the context of debt and money earned! There are also some great commercial games that help review integers and order of operations in a fun way. My favorites are the classic game of *24* and the new classic, *Absolute Zero* card game.

During the high school years, you still do not need to complicate mathematics. There are so many wonderful online classes, internet resources, traditional textbooks with DVD instruction and homeschool co-op classes to take. Remember, less is more, so don't give into the temptation of cramming every lesson into every day. If your teen needs more time to grapple with a new algebraic or geometric concept, then slow down and let him work at his own pace. If it is in your budget, consider one-on-one tutoring if math is not your strength. If your teen has a natural aptitude for mathematics and dreams of being an engineer, scientists, or doctor, then include four or five years of math in his high school years. However, if math is not one of your teen's strengths or she is going into a field that requires only basic math skills, consider doing only two or three years of math in high school. This way she can take her time, spend two years completing Algebra 1 while really learning to understand it.

If your teen is not interested in a math or scientific field, then include mathematical courses such as personal finance, economics, and business math instead of a year of trigonometry or calculus. No matter which profession your teen chooses, he will need to manage his own money as an adult. Another great way to incorporate math at the high school level is to allow your student to start her own business. Is she a talented dancer? Then she can teach tap at the local community center. Does she knit or sew? Then she can create an Etsy account to sell her products. Is she a natural with little kids? Homeschooling moms are always looking for helpers and babysitters. My daughter started her own cupcake business when she was twelve and used that money to help finance her first trip abroad in high school. She also loved photography, games, and dance so she taught three classes at our local homeschool co-op. The money she earned helped pay for her own

Personal Finance, Economics or Business Math should be included in a student's high school program.

private lessons in dance. My son started a Lego business when he was ten and as a teen, he taught a Lego class at our local homeschool group, which helped him save for his first car. He loves all things baseball so in middle school and high school, he helped his coach shag balls during baseball camps, helped sell concessions at the Saturday

Little League games, and helped with the Challenger league. Have your teens use the high school years to learn how to apply mathematical skills in the real world and how to make and manage their own money.

Remember, less is more even in the area of mathematics. Try not to let math get to you or frustrate your child. Don't push. Some kids were designed by God to have an analytical mind and some were designed to be more creative. If your child is not getting a new concept no matter how many times you explain it or how many times he tries to do it, he might not be mentally ready to understand that particular skill. Don't beat your head against the wall or ruin your relationship with your child over long division. Don't view the breakdown or frustration as an interruption. View it as God's new plans for your day (or month). Take a break from that mathematical concept for a few days or even a few weeks. Just like adults, kids need time to chew on a new concept. You might find that after a month of not drilling common denominators, your son finally gets it a few weeks later after a break from his fraction worksheets. Don't take a complete break from math, just take a break from the concepts that are causing problems. Instead of drilling ratios and proportions, spend a few weeks reviewing skills he has already mastered. This will give your child a sense of accomplishment instead of him constantly feeling like a math failure. Instead of doing extra worksheets on multi-digit multiplication, spend a few weeks playing math games to review math facts in a fun and engaging way.

The beauty of homeschooling is the freedom and flexibility to learn as a family. The one room school house concept is one of the easiest ways to incorporate this "Less is more and simple is better" way of thinking into teaching the humanities too. When homeschooling, especially during the wonder years, there really is no need to use formal social studies, history, or science textbooks. Pick one or two areas of science to dig into each year and learn the topics together as a family. As a family, pick one historical era and delve deep into that time period. As Charlotte Mason recommended, use Living Books to teach the humanities. Use biographies, non-fiction books, and classic novels to learn about a time period or a particular culture.

The beauty of homeschooling is the freedom and flexibility to learn as a family. The one room school house concept is one of the easiest ways to incorporate this "Less is more and simple is better" way of teaching.

Use picture books, encyclopedias, and biographies to learn about a particular area in science. If you are required to follow state standards, you can use the list of state standards as a guide to help you decide which history topics and science areas you will learn that year. If you are not required to follow state standards, then let your interests and your child's fascinations guide you in developing your humanities scope and sequence plan for the year.

When my daughter was around eight, she had two friends who were obsessed with American presidents. Even though the boys were four years apart, their mom spent an entire school year learning about the presidents. She started with George Washington and made her way to George Bush, the senior. They read biographies together. The older boy also read primary documents written or influenced by the president they were studying. The younger son would read something simpler like a picture book or a book from the *Who is series*. The boys were fascinated with the conflicts and wars that encumbered many of the presidents, so while they were learning about the president's life, they were also immersing themselves in the historical events of that time period. One boy had a knack for memorizing trivia so he spent most of his time learning trivial facts about each president and by default about many American wars. As a family, they memorized the presidents in order, reenacted famous presidential speeches, and played many board and card games with an American theme. Since we live in southern CA, they visited the presidential libraries in our state as well as many of the memorials and museums highlighting different wars or American heroes. That year they also planned a family vacation that included a trip to Washington D.C and to Mount Rushmore. Most of their writing revolved around research reports, book summaries, analysis of primary documents, and persuasive essays on historical speeches. My friend read books aloud at the older boy's academic level and tailored most of the activities to his skill level. Much to her surprise, the younger boy comprehended a lot more than she expected. He soaked it all in and could rattle off some presidential or war fact to an unsuspecting mom at park day. When needed, she watered down some of the activities for her younger son or added extra assignments for the older boy. They were learning as a family instead of parceling out the day between subjects and grade levels. I can guarantee that this family learned more about American history, the democratic process, and US presidents in one year than they would have learned separately by reading different social studies textbooks and answering end of the chapter comprehension questions.

Incorporate history whenever you can. When learning about a particular artist, learn about the time period in which he or she lived. What influenced his or her art work? See what was happening in other parts of the world during the

Incorporate the study of history whenever you can.

time the artist was living and creating. Who were his or her friends and contemporaries? In what country or area of the world did the artist live? Learn about that country and other influential people from that region. Do the same for musicians, scientists, and authors. Making connections between the person, his work, his motives, his background, and the time period in which he lived helps history come alive. When possible, go view work created by the artist, attend a concert playing the composer's music, visit a museum highlighting the author's life, or experiment with the scientific concepts the scientist discovered. Include Living Books and picture books into your study of art and music too.

For several years, we had a timeline that wrapped around our family room wall. It started with creation and ended with our birthdays. Each year as we studied a new time period, new artists and musicians, new Bible figures and Christian heroes, and new scientific topics, we added them to our timeline. The kids would take turns drawing an object that represented the event or the person we learned about on an index card. They would write the date and add a one or two word caption, such as the *Civil War* or *The Exodus*. It was a visual reminder that God's world is connected. (It was also a visual reminder to me on those days I felt like a homeschool failure. I could look up and see on the wall all of the learning that was really taking place.)

Every family is different and every family has their own homeschooling style, but I humbly suggest you incorporate Nature Studies as often as you can. In our homeschooling adventure, nature studies were always a big part of our journey. Even if you are not a

Charlotte Mason kind of girl, nature studies can be the easiest, cheapest, and best way to study science each and every year. Nature studies do not need to be fancy either. Actually when it comes to nature studies, less is more and simple is better!

We had a nature study backpack. We took it with us wherever we went even on field trips and to park days. In it, we had our nature journals or notebooks. We each had a nature journal including me. We also had in our backpack colored pencils, a magnifying glass, a few bug boxes, a clip board, binoculars, and a bunch of field guides. Nowadays, you can just use the internet to figure out what you saw or even better download an app to help you identify what you see as  you explore. Each week, we went on a hike, explored the backyard, went for a walk, or visited the zoo. Whatever we did, I just made sure I consistently planned to explore nature once a week. We would take our backpack and go! When we saw something that intrigued us, we sat down right there on the spot and drew it. Sometimes we would take a picture, so we could draw it or so we could look it up on the internet when we got home. Sometimes we would spend hours just

Nature studies can be the easiest, cheapest, and simplest way to study science each and every year.

sitting by a stream drawing a tree or drawing an interesting fungus that was growing out of a dead tree stump.

The best place to start doing nature studies is in your backyard. First, become experts on what is growing, living, and visiting your

Nature Study
Backpack:

1. Nature Journal
2. Colored Pencils
3. Magnifying Glass
4. Binoculars
5. Field Guides or app
6. camera or iphone

own backyard. Learn about the trees and flowers that grow in your backyard and in your neighborhood. Learn about the animals and insects that visit your backyard or live in your neighborhood. One month when my dad was living with us, his fascination for hummingbirds became our fascination. We set up hummingbird feeders everywhere. Since my dad could only sit in his wheelchair, we would set the feeders in places around our yard so we could see them through the windows. We would wait to see the hummingbirds flutter in our garden, drink from our fountain, or sip nectar from our flowers. We would count them, and my dad would tell them little tidbits about hummingbirds as they watched them eat. We also had a blue jay that would visit our yard every migration season. My dad would share his fascination with bird watching with my son as they watched Mr. Blue Jay perch on the branches of our myrtle tree.

You could literally spend a whole year studying, observing, and learning about the native plants and animals in your own backyard and neighborhood. With the abundance of wildlife in God's creation, you really don't need a formal science class or curriculum until your children hit high school. You can easily use nature studies every year for science. Actually, we even used nature studies for our high school biology studies. The possibilities are endless! God's creation abounds with creativity and wonder.

Don't abandon the "Less is More" mentality and one room school house when your teen enters high school. You can still learn history, science, and the humanities as a family even when your teen is in high school.   For example, when your teen is learning American Government, as a family you can also learn about the Declaration of Independence, The Constitution, the electoral college, and the law-making process.   As your teen is learning about a new topic, not only is he writing papers about it and reading primary documents on his own, but he can teach what he is learning to the rest of the family.

Jesus, our Master Teacher, taught the most important lessons in the simplest of ways.

Using this simple approach, you are no longer the main teacher, but your teen who is quickly becoming an expert on American politics and the American dream is the primary teacher. When your teen is doing independent research on the Colonial Era, read to the younger children books such as *Ben and Me* by Lawson, *Shhh, We are Writing the Constitution* by Fritz, *We the Kids: The Preamble to the Constitution* by Catrow, and *If You Sailed on the Mayflowe*r by McGovern. As a family, play games that teach about the Constitution in a fun way. Some of our family favorites are *The Constitution Quest*, *Hail to the Chief*, and *USA Edition of Monopoly*.

The key point to remember is no matter which approach you use, it doesn't have to be expensive or complicated. Jesus taught the most important lessons in the simplest of ways. He shared his heart. He asked questions. He expounded on God's Word. He taught through example. He used the world around him to teach important life lessons. He valued, loved, and nurtured his disciples. Yes, in today's day and age, we do have great resources available to us and if some of them make your life easier and help calm your self doubt, then use them. But you can also successfully homeschool using this "Less is More" attitude. Friend, you and I can do all things through Christ who strengthens us, including homeschooling our children.

CHAPTER 13
I: Internet (Unplug & Plug In!)

One of the best ways to simplify your life and homeschooling is to unplug every now and then. Kids need to be outside! Moms, this includes you too. We were designed to enjoy God's creation. Our bodies need the Vitamin D. We need the fresh air and the sweet songs of the birds singing in our ears. So I encourage you to unplug and go outside! Play outside. Do lessons outside. Read aloud outside. Go on hikes. Take walks. Climb trees. Get dirty. It's important we get outside and encourage our kids to play outside! Sadly, children and this iGeneration in particular have been staying indoors more than any other generation before. Since we can play virtually, socialize virtually, and learn virtually, kids, teens, and young adults are glued to their phones, iPads and computers screens. I'm not saying all technology is bad or that you should eliminate all screen time for your family. Technology, like everything else, is a good thing when consumed in moderation.

However, it can be physically and mentally unhealthy to be on our screens all day long. In Richard Louv's book, *Last Child in the*

Woods: Saving Our Children From Nature Deficit Disorder, he talks about how technology and our crazy schedules are causing our children to spend less time outside, how this is negatively affecting them, our families, and our society, and how we can shift this paradigm. It is a brilliant, articulate, and sobering book! It is now one of my favorites, and I recommend it to moms and homeschooling moms alike. We need to make time for kids to have unstructured play, to play outside, and to explore nature.

We need to unplug and then make sure we plug in! Oddly, with all of the conveniences that technology provides, more and more families find themselves busier than ever. The overuse of technology hasn't slowed down a person's day to day responsibilities and activities. Ironically, it has created a more hectic lifestyle for most of us. How many times have you said just this past week, "I don't have enough time in the day to get everything done?" In the past ten years, I have watched a new trend unfold in the homeschooling community. Families are so busy with outside classes

> *"In nature, a child finds freedom, fantasy, and privacy; a place distant from the adult world, a separate peace."*
> -Richard Louv

and indoor screen time that they do not have time to fellowship in person with friends and other homeschooling families. Not only do we need to unplug from our computer screens, but we need to be intentional about plugging into a community.

Go outside! Play outside. Do lessons outside. Read aloud outside. Go on hikes. Take walks. Climb trees. Get dirty.

Society's misconception that homeschoolers are unsocialized has been proven incorrect again and again. However, it is true that homeschooling moms need to be more intentional about creating time and space for building friendships. Since we homeschool, our children do not have those built-in "social hours" that brick and mortar schools provide. In many ways, institutionalized socialization with same-age peers is not healthy or needed. But our children do crave to find a soulmate or kindred spirit to learn with and hang out with. Moms, we need and crave this too! Let's be honest. As rewarding as homeschooling can be, it can also be a little lonely at times. We need to make time for fellowship opportunities. We need to plug in to a homeschool support group, a nature club, or a co-op. We need to plug in at church and in our community. We need to consistently attend park days with friends and go on field trips with our local homeschool groups. We need to attend mom night outs, women Bible studies, or book clubs. We can't do this alone. We shouldn't do this alone. Find a homeschool community that is made up of moms who share your values and who can lift you up, encourage you, and pray for you. The more you simplify your life, your commitments, and your calendars, the more time you will have to fellowship with friends. Truly, one of the easiest ways to simplify your life and your homeschooling is to unplug and then plug in.

Chapter 14
F: Flexibility is Key

Blessed are the flexible, for they shall not be broken. This was one of my dad's favorite expressions. I am one of the least flexible persons I know (and I mean that literally and figuratively). I hate interruptions. I hate when things don't go as planned. I hate when our plans change. My more flexible and spontaneous friends view interruptions or cancelations as excursions, adventures, and new opportunities for learning. Sadly, I don't have the same attitude although I wish I did. My lack of flexibility and ability to change course has broken me more times than I can count. It is something the Lord and I have been working on for years. While I am better about seeing interruptions as God appointments and cancelations as extra time for something more important, I still have a very long way to go in being more flexible!

God has taught me many valuable lessons over the years as He has been stretching me and helping me become more flexible. One very important lesson I have learned and come to whole-heartedly embrace is that it is acceptable to change course. Someone once told me, "If Plan A doesn't work, then there are 25 other letters in the alphabet I could use! This was mind-blowing to me. Not only was it ok to change course if something wasn't working in our homeschooling, but there were many other ways to proceed. Don't be afraid to stop or take a break from using a particular curriculum or approach. I have a closet full of books I used with my daughter. They worked so well with her, that I saved them so when my son was old enough, we could use the same great books. Ha! If you have been homeschooling for a while, you know where I am going with this. Every last bit of saved curriculum was eventually donated. None of it worked with my son. The ones my daughter loved the most were the ones my son hated. What works for one student may not work for another. We have to be willing to try something new. We have to be flexible enough to give up something that may have worked before but isn't working now.

"Blessed are the flexible, for they shall not be broken."

- Unknown

Don't be afraid to take a break. It may not be the curriculum you are using or the class your son is taking. It might be that he is just not mentally ready to learn a particular concept. Before ditching an entire curriculum, set it aside for a few weeks. Try something new.

Break up the monotony. You may be in a rut. Your son might need a mental break. Do something completely different for a while or take a break from that academic subject altogether for a few weeks. When tensions have calmed, the chaos has been removed, and the tantrums have subsided, then try it again. Chances are when you return to the concept, the mental fog will be lifted, and you can begin to once again successfully teach or use whatever you were doing before.

However if the frustration or tears return after taking a break, then pray about changing what you are doing and using. If you do decide you need a new approach or a new curriculum, first try borrowing it before making a huge purchase. You may find the curriculum that comes so highly recommended is perfect for your friend and her family, but it does not work for you or your family. And that is ok! On the flip side, you may find the new books or different curriculum recommended are an answer to prayer. In that case, do an about face, change direction, and dive into something new. After

If you become a slave to your curriculum guide, you are giving away your freedom to educate your child the way you feel is best for him or her.

twenty plus years of eclectic homeschooling, I have tried and used just about everything out there. I binge buy when frustrations are high.

I tend to drop everything in the winter when we hit the "February Wall" and enter "March Madness." I have come to realize certain methods may work for one season but not for another. I have come to understand that certain curriculums may work some years for one child but fail miserably the next year. As homeschooling moms, we need to seek God's wisdom on when to stay the course, when to change course, and when to just get out of the boat altogether!

Another important lesson God has taught me is that each child is unique, fearfully, and wonderfully made. This may have been a lesson I already knew but for some reason, I need God to remind me of this often. During my first year of teaching fifth graders, my teaching supervisor told me to always remember that we teach children not curriculum. Our goal should not be to check off all of the boxes, but to nurture the child God has put in our care. Our goal isn't to fill their brains with important information they may need for some test or for some college course. Our goal is to whet their appetite for the things of God, to plant seeds of curiosity that hopefully will bloom

Certain methods may work for one season of homeschooling but not for another. Seek God's wisdom on when to stay the course, when to change course, or when to just get out of the boat for a while.

later in life, and to give them the tools to find information on their own when needed. Our goal should be to raise life-long learners not scholarship recipients.

If you use a standard curriculum, then make sure your relationship with your teacher's guide is a healthy one. The teacher's guide is a manual filled with ideas to help *guide* you. It is not a set of instructions you have to blindly follow. Its sole purpose is to help you. Don't feel like you

"When Plan A doesn't work, there are 25 other letters in the alphabet to work with."

- Unknown

have to do every activity, read every page, and answer every question suggested in the guide. They are *suggestions*. Don't be a slave to whatever curriculum or methodology you are using. Embrace the freedom and flexibility that comes with the privilege of homeschooling. When you become a slave to a curriculum, a teacher's guide, a set of state standards, or a mandated school schedule, you are giving away your freedom to educate your child the way you feel is best for him or her. *Blessed are the flexible, for they shall not be broken.* If it is necessary, add this to your list of beatitudes. It truly is a blessing to be flexible. You may finish this homeschooling race a little bruised, but you won't be broken if you have the courage and obedience to bend to God's will and His plans for you and your family.

CHAPTER 15
Y: Your Ultimate Job Description

When I became a mom, I wished someone would have sat me down, looked me straight in the eyes, and told me the truth: "Honey, you may not survive this!" It's true. Motherhood is hard. It is a blessing and by far the best job I have ever had. I would not trade this ministry of motherhood for anything. But the truth is, it is hard. When you add homeschooling on top of keeping everyone mentally, physically, emotionally, and spiritually safe, the mission becomes even more challenging. I'm not going to sugar coat it. If you have chosen to accept this mission of homeschooling, you might develop a few little tics. Your eyes might start to twitch. You might find yourself aimlessly rocking back and forth for no reason at all. You may have menopausal symptoms all the time no

Being a homeschool mom is a blessing, a privilege, a calling, and a gift, but it can also be hard.

matter what stage of life you are in. You may become an insomniac. You will definitely stress eat. You may find gray hair at an alarming rate. You will yell for all kinds of reasons and find most of those reasons weren't logical ones. You may laugh until you cry and cry until you laugh, and there is a good chance there will be days that you look and sound like the crazy cat lady who constantly talks to everyone and no one in particular. Being a homeschooling mom is a blessing, a privilege, a calling, and a gift, but it can also be hard.

When I meet with moms who are new to homeschooling, I try to speak words of encouragement to them while being completely honest. I tell them, "You can do this, and you will love it! You will be there for the most important 'ah ha' moments, and you will be the first person they want to share an accomplishment with. In the end, you

God calls us to be faithful disciples not phenomenal teachers or perfect moms.

will have a strong relationship with your children, and they will rise up and call you blessed. But there will be hard days, hard weeks, and sometimes hard seasons, but you can do this!" I wholeheartedly declare this to you too. Moms, we've got this! We can do this. God has called us to this, therefore, He will make it possible.

In order to enjoy the journey, we need to make sure we understand our job description. God calls us to be faithful disciples, not phenomenal teachers or perfect moms. Did you catch that? This is not in the fine print of your contract, but it is in the red letters of the Bible. God calls us to be faithful. *"He who is faithful in what is least is faithful also in much"* (Luke 16:10). God blesses those who remain faithful. *"A faithful man will abound with blessings"* (Proverbs 28:20). God rewards faithfulness. *"His Lord said to him, 'Well done, good and faithful servant; you were faithful over a few things, I will make you ruler over many things. Enter into the joy of your Lord'"* (Matthew 25:21). Proverbs 31: 10-31 lists the faithful actions

Your child is exactly where God wants him to be. God has a master plan for you child. It is a mighty and awesome plan, and you are a major part of that God-ordained plan.

of a noble woman and a godly mother. She is faithful in the tasks God has given her. She is a model to us on how to be a faithful disciple.

God doesn't expect perfection; He seeks transformation. *"Being confident of this, that He who began a good work in you will carry it on to completion until the day of Christ Jesus"* (Philippians 1:6). God isn't finished with us yet. Friend, like Gideon, God sees you and me not as we are today, but as He has created us to be. Gideon saw himself as weak and unworthy of the task God called him to, but God saw him as a mighty warrior worthy of the task set before him. We can claim God's promise to Gideon for ourselves. *"Mighty hero, the*

Lord is with you" (Judges 6: 12). The Lord called us to homeschool, therefore, He will be with us every step of the way. His mighty army will go before us. His cleft is our refuge.

While our job description is the same, each of us are called to complete this mission in different ways. God created each of us with our own set of gifts and passions. The way you homeschool will look different from the way I homeschool. Because we are uniquely made and gifted, we should stop comparing ourselves, our families, and our homeschooling to others who have been given this job as well. Don't compare! Don't play the comparison game. When you read homeschooling books or when you talk with other homeschooling moms at events or park days, use what they are sharing as a resource, not as a litmus test of how you're doing. Talk to other moms. Get ideas from other moms. Share your concerns with other homeschooling moms. But don't leave a coffee date, a homeschool conference, or a park day feeling defeated. Don't be afraid to be you and to teach in a way that is comfortable for

Because we are uniquely created and gifted, we should not compare ourselves, our families, or our homeschooling to others who have also been called to homeschool.

you. God gave you a particular skill set and personality. Use your passions and fascinations to teach what you love.

Don't fall into the trap of comparing yourself and your homeschool style with others. God gave you your children on purpose! If God wanted your kids to be taught just like your "picture perfect" homeschool friend down the street, He would have given your friend custody of your children. God knew there was no one else who would love, understand, and support your child

"No eye has seen, no ear has heard, no mind has conceived what God has prepared for those who love him."

1 Corinthians 2:9

like you do. God knew there is no one else who wants your child to succeed as much as you do. God knew there is no one else who will pray for your child like you do! Your child is exactly where God wants him to be. God has a master plan for your child. It is a mighty and awesome plan and you, my friend, are a major part of that God-ordained plan. Remember, your ultimate job description is to be a faithful disciple not a perfect mom. However, I can say with complete confidence that you are the perfect person for the job!

"A faithful man [and woman] will abound with blessings."

Proverbs 28:20

CONCLUSION

So friend, *just breathe*! Take another deep breath and take another sip of coffee. You've got this! It is my prayer that you and I will be blessed beyond measure as we apply the Principles of the Sabbath and the Principles of Simplification to our ministry of motherhood and our calling to homeschool. It is my prayer that our homes and our homeschools will be God-honoring, Christ-centered, and Spirit-filled. Breathe with a little more ease today. Take heart, my friend. Rest in the assurance that *"No eye has seen, no ear has heard, no mind has conceived what God has prepared for those who love him"* (1 Corinthians 2:9). God has prepared plans for you and for your children, plans that are far better and far richer than anything we can even imagine. We can breathe with confidence because we stand on God's promises. May God richly bless your homeschool adventure for His glory.

Chapter
Personal Reflection
& Discussion
Questions

Coffee Break
Sabbath Day

What can you begin to do to truly honor the Sabbath each week?

How can you reorganize your schedule in order to use the Principle of Double Portions in your homeschooling?

Coffee Break
Sabbath Hour

What might an hour of rest each day look like for you?

| |
| |
| |
| |
| |
| |

Keeping the ages of your children in mind, what might an hour of rest look like for each of your children?

| |
| |
| |
| |
| |
| |
| |

Coffee Break
Sabbath Week

Chapter 3

If the idea of taking a whole week off every six weeks scares you, list your objections.

Every six weeks, what can your family do (or not do) in order to rest, rejuvenate and/or refocus?

Coffee Break
Sabbath Year

If you have been homeschooling for a while, have you ever had to take an extended break from homeschooling? Think about that time or that year. List all of the ways God provided for you and for your family during that time and how God blessed your family and homeschooling during that year.

**If you are new to homeschooling, think of a time God gave you an extended time to rest.

Coffee Break
Daily Sabbath

Chapter 5

When do you have your personal quiet time with the Lord? What does it look like?

How can you rearrange your day, your schedule, or your priorities to make sure you have a "Coffee Date" with Jesus each day?

Coffee Break
Sabbath Margins

What items or subjects would you like to do daily as a family and include in your "Morning Time" or Family Time Basket?

What items, subjects, or activities do you "never get to" that you would like to make time for by rotating into your morning time or family time?

Coffee Break
S.i.m.p.l.i.f.y

What items or "rocks" are in your cart (or minivan) that God has given you to do?

What items or "rocks" are in your cart (or minivan) that you keep adding but may not necessarily be God-given? What "rocks" can you remove this season?

Coffee Break
Start With the End in Mind

Why do you want to homeschool? Write your family's Homeschool Mission Statement.

| |
| |
| |
| |
| |
| |

Meditate on God's Word. Find a verse you feel God is calling your family to obey or a promise to claim. Make it this year's theme verse for your family and for your homeschooling.

Coffee Break
Invite Others Along

Chapter 9

List events and activities both you and your children can consistently participate in to build community and lasting friendships.

| |
| |
| |
| |
| |
| |

Which adults in your life and in your child's life can you include in your homeschooling? Which adults can mentor your teen or share their passions and gifts with your youngster?

| |
| |
| |
| |
| |
| |

How are you (or your child's school) getting in the way of his/her education?

What do you consider to be the most important things your child needs to learn? How can you be more intentional about including opportunities to learn those things?

List all of the activities you do outside of the home?

Look at your list. Which ones are necessary? Which ones bring you joy? Which ones cause stress or financial burdens? Prayerfully consider which ones God is calling you to eliminate (even if it is just for a season.)

Coffee Break
Less is More

What subjects or topics can you learn this year as a family? List out historical eras, scientific topics, art & musical periods, and/or skills (like watercolor, dance, instrument, knitting, etc) you want to learn as a family.

What subjects can you cover just once or twice a week?

Coffee Break
Unplug & Plug In

Chapter 13

List activities your children can do daily or weekly that encourages them to get outdoors and/or to be creative.

What do you love about your homeschooling community? With whom do you do life? With whom can you learn? Pray about starting a co-op with a small group of friends. What could you do and/or learn together?

Coffee Break
Flexibility is Key

Chapter 14

What is your relationship like with your teacher's guide (and/or state standards)? Are you a slave to your "To Do List" or is it a guide for your day?

How are you your worst enemy? What are some things (or expectations that you have) that torpedo your homeschooling efforts? What can you give to God and what can you do differently?

Coffee Break
Your Ultimate Job Description

List all of the blessings of being a mom. List all of the blessings you have experienced because you are a homeschooling mom.

What makes YOU the perfect person to teach your child?

Notes

Notes

RESOURCES

Introduction:

1. "Breathe" written by Johnny Diaz from the album *Everything is Changing* © 2015

Chapter 3 Sabbath Week: A Week of Rest

1. *Teaching From Rest: A Homeschooler's Guide to Unshakeable Peace* (2015) written by Sarah Mackenzie and published by Classical Academic Press. The idea of taking a week off every six weeks comes from this book and Classical Conservations.™

2. Bible Study Fellowship (BSF) is an international, intergenerational Bible study that uses a four fold approach to studying God's Word. Their weekly discussion questions for adults and children can be used for family devotions, Bible studies, and/or Bible curriculum.

3. *One Year Sports Devotions for Kids* (2011) by Jesse Florea.

Chapter 6 Sabbath Margins: Extra Wiggle Room

1. *Teaching From Rest: A Homeschooler's Guide to Unshakeable Peace* 2015 written by Sarah Mackenzie and published by Classical Academic Press. The idea of planning with margins comes from this book.

2. *Better Together* (2018) written by Pam Barnhill and *A Handbook to Morning Time* (2016) written by Cindy Rollins. The idea of Morning Time comes from Cindy Rollin's book and is further explained by Pam Barnhill's book and podcast.

3. *Your Morning Time Basket* website and podcast by Pam Barnhill (https://pambarnhill.com)

Chapter 7 S.i.m.p.l.i.f.y Acronym

1. This story of the "Man and the Oxcart" is based on a story shared in *Having a Mary Heart in a Martha World* (2000) written by Joanna Weaver.

2. S.I.M.P.L.I.F.Y acronym was created by Carrie De Francisco and shared at annual weekend for homeschooling moms, Healthy Homeschooling" in 2018.

Chapter 8 S: Start With the End in Mind

1. The phrase "Start with the end in mind" comes from Carol Joy Seid's seminar "Begin With the End in Mind" (https://www.carolejoyseid.com)

2. *DK's Illustrated Family Bible* (2013) published by DK Publishing

3. *The Child's Story Bible* by Catherine Vos (1983)

4. *God's Amazing Creatures and Me* by Helen Haidle (2000)

5. *The Big Book of Animal Devotions* by William Coleman (2009)

6. *Window on the World: When We Pray, God Works* by Daphne Spraggett (2007)

Chapter 10 M: Mark Twain's Motto

1. *The Successful Homeschool Family Handbook* (1994) written by Dr. Raymond Moore

2. Research on brain development and advantage of play provided by Dr. Karyn Purvis, "The Benefits of Play in Cognitive Development" (https://child.tcu.edu/)

3. Many of the games suggested came from *The Games Curriculum* created by Martin and Carolyn Forte (https://gamecurriculum.com)

4. *Gameology Class*, FUNdamentals Wednesday Classes, Monrovia, CA

Chapter 12   L: Less Is More

1. *Better Late Than Early* by Dr. Raymond Moore (1989)

2. *Teaching Arithmetic: Lessons for Decimals and Percents (2002)* by Carrie De Francisco and Marilyn Burns. Many of the fraction and decimal suggestions were taken from this book.

3. *Math FUNdamentals:Using Games to Teach Math* (2006) by Carrie De Francisco (out of print). Many of the games and suggestions were taken from this book.

4. *The Philosophy of Education: The Home Education Series* (2017) by Charlotte Mason. The idea of using Living Books, Print Studies, Composer Studies and Nature Studies were taken from this book and others in this series.

5. "The Literature Based Approach to Education" seminar by Carol Joy Seid. The application of using Living Books to teach the humanities in part came from this seminar. (https://www.carolejoyseid.com)

Chapter 13   I: Internet (Unplug and Plug In!)

1. *Last Child in the Woods: Saving Our Children From Nature Deficit Disorder* (2008) Richard Louv

2. *The Call of the Wild and Free: Reclaiming Wonder in Your Child's Education* (2019) by Ainsley Arment

About The Author

Mistakenly, many of my friends insist my children have been successful on this homeschooling journey *because* I am a credentialed teacher. This statement could not be farther from the truth! I have learned many valuable lessons as a homeschooling mom, but three lessons stand out the most. First, anyone can homeschool if one is called to do so and if she relies on God for strength and guidance. Second, you must have a sense of humor to be a wife, a mother, and a homeschooling mom. And finally, no one can teach their child better than a child's mom (or primary caregiver). These are things no college degree or teaching credential can teach a person.

After all of these years, I can honestly say homeschooling has been an adventure and a blessing for our family. The most important credential on my resume is not my BS in Science, my MA in Education, or my CA teaching credential. It isn't that I am an author, a certified IEW writing instructor, or former adjunct professor. It isn't that my husband and I run a successful homeschool co-op and weekly homeschool classes for over 175 families. In the grand scheme of life and in homeschooling, none of those things really matter. My most important credential is that through the power of the Holy Spirit and the grace of Jesus Christ, I am a child of God, a much-loved wife, and a free-spirited homeschooling mom. When I am asked what I do for a living, I humbly respond, "I homeschool my kids and help others do the same."

Originally from New Orleans, LA, Carrie De Francisco is now living, loving, and learning in Southern California with her husband, Mike, her two children, Francesca and Joseph, and their introverted dog, Jesse.

About Coffee With Carrie

Coffee With Carrie is a Christian ministry dedicated to encouraging and equipping homeschooling moms to educate their children at home using biblical principles and simple and stress-free methods.

Coffee With Carrie Podcast and Website offer homeschooling advice, tips, and ideas to support, encourage, and edify moms who are called to this adventure of homeschooling. *Coffee With Carrie* also offers consulting services, online seminars, and special weekend events for homeschooling moms to support, encourage, and edify moms who are educating their children at home. To listen or subscribe to *Coffee With Carrie* Podcast, visit https://www.buzzsprout.com/939064 or find her on iTunes and Spotify.

Coffee With Carrie can also be found on Instagram where she offers daily devotions, homeschooling tips, and a bit of coffee humor. To find Carrie on Instagram, check out @coffeewithcarrieconsultant.

For more information on *Coffee With Carrie,* upcoming Special Weekends for Homeschooling Moms, or Carrie's availability for speaking, visit www.coffeewithcarrie.org or https://linktr.ee/coffeewithcarrieconsultant

"All our children shall be taught by the Lord, and great shall be the peace of our children." Isaiah 54:13

Acknowledgments

I could not have gotten through the editing process without Georgina Tanefski. Thank you for your help and for your years of friendship. I am so grateful the Lord brought our girls together so many years ago at Bible study. You are a gift to me and to our family.

I would like to thank Francesca and Joseph for their creative input and help with the cover design. Your eye for detail and photo editing skills helped bring my vision to life.

A huge thank you to my husband, Michael, for taking over the mounds of laundry and house cleaning when I was knee-deep in writing and editing. I could not have done this without you.

I also have a heart full of gratitude for homeschooling mentors like Carolyn and Martin Forte who have talked me off a few homeschooling cliffs and for my homeschooling friends and community who have walked this homeschooling journey with me, encouraged me, prayed with me, prayed for me, and put up with me.

Finally, a huge shout out to my brother, Frank Mayeur. His humor and timely phone calls and texts were always just what I needed. You rock!